A Young Man in the
Wild Blue Yonder

Thoughts of a B-25 Pilot
In World War II

David K. Hayward

Table of Contents

Introduction   i
1.   My First Combat Mission   1
2.   The Big Decision   7
3.   Appointment With Destiny   13
4.   See America First   19
5.   Encountering Ack Ack   23
6.   At Santa Ana   27
7.   Boondoggle Over Tibet   33
8.   The Wild Blue Yonder   39
9.   No Longer a Dodo   47
10. Wendell Hanson   55
11. Basic Flying School   63
12. An Upperclassman   69
13. Assignment at Dinjan   77
14. Advanced Flying School   85
15. Cross Country Flying   91
16. Between Assignments   101
17. The B-25 Mitchell Bomber   105
18. Analyzing the Crash   113
19. Target Practice   121
20. On the Way to the CBI   127
21. Settling In at Chakulia   137
22. Flying from Chakulia   147
23. Over the Hump to China   157
24. A Different Kind of Target   165
25. Mission to Tourane (Da Nang)   175
26. Those Who Didn't Make It   183

27. Departing from Yangkai   189
28. Leave and Reassignment   191
29. The Nation's Capital   195
30. Flying Different Planes   201
31. Flying the VIPs   209
32. The War Was Over   217
33. Wilmer McDowell—Reunions   221
34. Return to China in 1989   229
35. A Veterans' Tour to China   235
36. Return in 2004 and 2005   239
37. My Sixth Return   247
38. What Happened to Them?   253
39. Closing Comments   261
Acknowledgments   263
Sources   265

Introduction

WHY WOULD A 91-year-old veteran of World War II take on the job of writing a book about his war experiences seventy years ago? Where would he find the details necessary to make an accurate and cohesive story? Memory alone would not be enough.

The answer? Most of the writing has been done. It was a matter of putting the pieces together, like a jigsaw puzzle. My diary, written in 1942, covered the years of entering the war and the training that followed. My photo album provided illustrations and comments. Add to that my pilot's log book, military orders, letters, and official records of the 22nd Bomb Squadron from Maxwell Air Force Base in Montgomery, Alabama, and much more.

One day in the year 1990 my telephone rang. The caller was Ted Kratzke, a veteran of the 22nd Bomb Squadron. Ted asked, "Are you the same David Hayward who was in the 22nd Bomb Squadron in the China-Burma-India Theater?" I replied that I was. He continued, "I have been looking for you."

After a friendly chat he told me a group of 22nd Bomb Squadron veterans met for a reunion in St. Louis, Missouri, in 1987 and planned to meet again in Reno, Nevada, later that year. He asked, "Would you be able to attend? Can I put your name on the mailing list?"

I eagerly replied, "Count me in."

The reunion had an impact on me. Lloyd Klar, one of our veterans who was a personnel manager for Dow Chemical Company and possessed a most persuasive manner, asked me if I'd be willing to serve the group as secretary. Well, I had recently retired from my career as a petroleum engineer and did have the time to take on a new assignment, so I agreed to. Then I thought, *If I'm serving as secretary, the job will flow more efficiently if I were treasurer as well.* The position soon became secretary-treasurer. Further, I continued thinking, *I should write a newsletter to help generate interest among the veterans, their families, and friends.*

Over time, as the veterans sent in their dues and comments, they also sent stories of their wartime experiences. *Why not combine those stories into book form?* I thought. With the Board of Governors' approval and help from other key veterans, I arranged their stories in chronological order and published the anthology entitled "Eagles, Bulldogs & Tigers." The name represents the three logos of our squadron in the China-Burma-India Theater. At first we were the Flying Eagles. Later the name changed to Bombing Bulldogs. When the squadron moved from India to China, we became part of the Flying Tigers of the 14th Air Force, commanded by General Claire Chennault. Thus the title "Eagles, Bulldogs & Tigers" evolved.

Another book followed, using more stories contributed by talented story tellers in the squadron. "WWII DIARY" was uniquely illustrated with caricatures by John A. Johns, one of our pilots and a gifted artist. His work appears in this book as well. Our Board of Governors encouraged members to submit their stories, not only for "WWII DIARY", but also for our quarterly newsletters. As a contributor myself, I wrote several articles describing my wartime experiences. Those are a large part of this book.

Thursday, May 14, 1942

134th day — 231 days follow

I soloed today ! ! !
Ah! What a thrill! It
really seemed great to be the
master of the ship for a
change. At times I kind of
missed that head and shoulders
up front, but really it was
much easier to be the sole
operator. Somehow, I had the
idea I was flying an old "blimp,"
but still it was fun. The
takeoffs & landings were
much better than I had
ever done before, but I guess
that is the way it always
goes.

Friday, May 15, 1942

135th day — 230 days follow

My instructor was absent
today, so the Flight Commander
took over. He gave me some very
good criticism concerning my
flying which I have been
wondering about for some time.
He said I make the mistake
of flying "just well enough to
get there", and that I do not
always strive for perfection. He
says he knows I can do it
well whenever he asks me
specially, but on the whole
I have a tendency to gold-
brick. If this is so, it
is certainly not intentional,
but anyway, I now have
something to work on.

David Hayward's 1942 diary

CHAPTER 1
My First Combat Mission

THAT FIRST COMBAT MISSION, of which I thought would be my last, was on April 8, 1943. All new pilots were required to split their crews for the first few missions so they'd all gain experience with seasoned combat crews. I flew as copilot that day with Lt. Loyal G. Brown as pilot, who had flown about 40 combat missions by that time. We called him by his first two initials, "LG".

Our formation of ten B-25 medium bombers took off before sunrise so that we'd get back before the afternoon thunderstorms set in. LG brought our plane into formation and kept sight of the running lights on the other planes, maintaining an easterly course. Our V formation had three flights of three planes each, with the tenth plane forming a diamond at the end of the line. With no fighter escort in those early months, we depended on the concentration of fire power from gunners in a tight formation, in the event of attack by enemy fighters. Radio silence was essential until after the bomb run; by then we'd be returning to our base.

The sun came up as our squadron crossed the Chin Hills into Burma. Gunners test-fired their guns and pilots tightened up the formation. Our commanding officer, flying in the lead ship, took us to the bombing run at Meiktila airdrome in central Burma; here our bombardiers dropped all bombs on a signal from the lead ship. Then the pilots headed for home. Normally that was a happy time, the day's first real feeling of relief. Even the sandwiches tasted good, though I always wondered if those black specks in the bread were bugs of some kind. Indeed, usually they were. Bread was baked at night when insects flew abundantly throughout the kitchen.

Our assigned airplane, with its number 13 painted on the nose wheel for identification, flew at the end of the formation in the "Tail End Charlie" spot. Not only that, our plane was a little slower at maximum speed than the rest of the formation, having recently been restored from a belly landing (without landing gear in place).

After the cry of "Bombs Away" came over the interphone system, I looked down from my copilot's window and saw other aircraft. They were not ours. I picked up my microphone and tried to report what I saw; however, other voices dominated the radio, reporting the same thing. A few minutes later I looked down again. The enemy airplanes were still in sight below us and traveling in the same direction as we were, but gaining altitude. Excited confusion crackled on the radio. I counted 21 Japanese airplanes—both fighters and bombers. Our lead pilot pushed his throttles forward and we did too, but our plane could not keep up with the others. Our leader must not have been aware of our vulnerable situation, a straggler in the midst of enemy fighter planes.

Our turret gunner called on the interphone. A Zero was doing a slow roll in the blind spot of our twin tail assembly where our guns were designed not to fire. The top turret of the B-25-C model was mounted further aft than on the later J model, so our large twin vertical stabilizers blanked out a larger field of fire than the later model would have. Japanese fighter pilots probably knew that and preferred to attack a B-25 from the rear.

Next I saw a Zero pulling into view from my copilot's window, just out of effective range of the turret gunner. The sight was shocking. Was this the end? As I looked at the Japanese airplane I couldn't help but wonder if that pilot could be a young fellow like me. Did he interrupt his education and go through similar training as mine? Here we were looking at each other. Thoughts shifted uneasily to an earlier day, less harried, when I weighed the options of whether to enlist or seek a deferment at a defense plant. *Perhaps I should have gone to work for Lockheed,* I thought half seriously.

In those fleeting moments I realized there are important things to worry about and unimportant things; this was clearly one of the important things. I swore that if I were to survive this I would never again worry about the unimportant.

What happened next was something I did not expect. The Japanese plane went away. Neither of our planes had fired a shot. He must have returned to his primary duty of protecting his bombers. LG kept flying westward toward home at full throttle. But at that setting our plane was running short on fuel and it could not make the long flight back to Chakulia.

The British base at Chittagong, India (now Bangladesh) lay just ahead, where we hoped to refuel. But as LG called in for landing instructions the control tower informed us the field was under a red alert and they expected an air raid, so the field was closed.

LG replied, "We have no choice; we are coming in whether there is a red alert or not."

Upon landing, a British officer drove out and ordered, "Proceed to Dum Dum airport, Calcutta, and do your refueling there." We did so with nearly empty tanks.

LG returned us to Chakulia and he reported our story to the debriefing officer, who replied nonchalantly, "Your experience was all in a day's work." I pondered: *If the missions ahead are to be anything like this, I'll never make it home.*

Wendell Hanson was a good friend who had trained with me. We flew to India in the same transport plane and he was aboard another plane in our formation on that mission. This was his recollection of the encounter:

I was copilot to Capt. Clarke Johnston. On the bombing run heading east we saw a very unusual formation. Thirty miles north of us, heading west at our altitude was a flight of Japanese twin engine bombers escorted by fighters. About 1,000 yards out, a Zero followed our formation but made no attempt to attack. Our lead radio operator warned India headquarters of the impending attack.

Why did the Japanese spare us that day? I've tried to figure it out since then. Was someone praying for us? Were the Japs stupid? Were we just plain lucky? Any of those are possible. Probably, I thought, we arrived at the Meiktila airdrome just after the Japanese took off on their mission to India, most likely to attack the installations at Chittagong. The Japanese fighter pilots must have been ordered to protect their bombers and not let a possible decoy distract them. Or they might have been concerned about the condition of their airfield at Meiktila which we just bombed. Or perhaps, because they lost the element of surprise, they wisely cancelled their mission for the day. If the situation were reversed, I wondered if our fighters would have taken the initiative to destroy as many enemy bombers as possible, certainly the straggling number 13.

I met LG again at a reunion of veterans at Rapid City, South Dakota, in 1992 and we have been in contact ever since. I asked him about his recollection of that mission and he replied:

It happened in 1943, around 13,000 feet and north of a place called Meiktila on the Irrawaddy River in Burma. Before takeoff from Chakulia, India, I requested a change in assigned planes, knowing the assigned one was the slowest in the squadron. The commanding officer, who was leading the flight, denied my request, saying that air discipline would keep order. I knew that our plane position would be the lowest in the formation and I would need more power to stay in formation.

After "Bombs Away" the lead plane speeded up and left us, "Low Joe", behind. We were flying three ships in three V's, javelin down, with our ship at the tail end. Suddenly, the rest of the squadron was only a speck in the distance; we could not raise radio contact with them.

Appearing off to our side and even with us was a Jap Zero. No fire, just a wave. We didn't fire and neither did he. I can see now in my memory how that red ball (rising sun) on the Jap plane fuselage was the biggest thing I had ever seen. As pilot I was sweating as though in a steam bath.

We made it to Chittagong on the Bay of Bengal in India, an Indian-British air base. I had barely shut the engines down when a British officer ordered us to depart regardless of the little gas we had, as the Jap fleet that we ran from was headed toward Chittagong. We left in a hurry for Dum Dum air base, Calcutta.

The rest of our flight was there at Dum Dum. I had a heated discussion with our flight leader and I could have been in deep trouble for my go at him, but it was never mentioned again. I was angry and did not discuss the situation with my crew. Whether our turret gunner had a reasonable shot at the Zero is unknown but evidently he did not.

After the war, Japanese records showed that the 50th Sentai (equivalent to an Air Force Group in the U.S.) was based at Meiktila at the time of our mission. They were equipped with Ki-43 Oscars, evidently the type of Zero fighter plane we encountered. The Japanese bombers we saw were probably Ki-21 Sallys, also active in the area at that time.

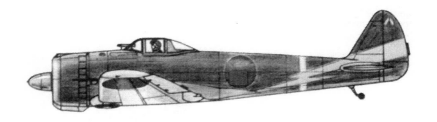

A Ki-43 Oscar of the 50th Sentai (Group) in Burma

After that flight, the ground looked very attractive.

CHAPTER 2
The Big Decision

As PRESIDENT FRANKLIN D. ROOSEVELT so eloquently put it, December 7, 1941, was "a date which will long live in infamy," the date that the Imperial Japanese bombed Pearl Harbor and other military installations resulting in our entry into World War II.

Where was I at the time? Our family lived in Pasadena, California, on a wide, tree-lined avenue. Our house was built by my grandfather, John Kirkland Hayward, in the 1920's, the second house to be constructed on our block. At the time of Pearl Harbor, our family consisted of my father, my brother Stewart who was four years my senior, and me, a 19-year-old, shy, awkward teenager. My mother died when I was only three years old and my father was quickly burdened by having to care for his aging father and handicapped brother, Jack, who suffered from rickets, a vitamin-deficiency illness that was a problem in those days. During my father's most difficult days, my brother Stewart and I were cared for at the Masonic Home in Covina, California, and later with a family at a foster home in Pasadena. By the time I reached third grade, my grandfather and Uncle Jack had passed away; and Stewart and I came back to live with our dad.

We were not wealthy; my father described our financial situation as "comfortable," thanks to funds his father had set aside. My father told me we were living on a budget of about $100 per month which, most of the time, we could live within. A hamburger cost ten cents and a movie not much more than that. Stewart and I each had jobs. I was a newspaper delivery boy,

7

which covered my personal expenses. It deprived me of early morning sleep, but it was good exercise to ride my bike with a heavy load of papers on the handle bars.

Movies were my favorite form of entertainment; I saw everything having to do with flying. How many times did James Cagney or Pat O'Brien recover from a tail spin just in time to avoid crashing into the earth below? The bad guy always got what he deserved and the pretty girl ended up with the good guy, which whetted my appetite for the adventure of flying.

At age 19, I graduated from Pasadena Junior College with an Associate of Arts degree in Economics. I drove a 1934 Ford V-8 that I loved, which allowed me to work at Fletcher Aircraft Schools in Burbank, California, earning 50 cents per hour. After what seemed like an eternity, I finally got a 10% raise to 55 cents per hour. Whoopee!

Fletcher was just down the road from the Lockheed aircraft plant where Hudson bombers and P-38 fighters were coming off the assembly line heading for Britain, Russia, and our own meager Army Air Corps. I fantasized about flying a P-38 myself someday. Indeed, I did in 1945, and it was one of the greatest thrills of my life. Back in 1942 a good friend of mine, Marshal Christen, had an older brother who held a responsible position at Lockheed. He arranged for a small group of us to visit the Lockheed plant, and even the Howard Hughes plant where Hughes was building his famous racer at the time. That whetted my appetite even more.

Our family was very conscious of war conditions leading up to Pearl Harbor. Over breakfast, the local Pasadena Star News brought us the latest developments. England had been at war since 1939, her army driven from the continent at Dunkirk. Her population endured horrible bombing during the Battle of Britain. German submarines devastated her supplies in the Atlantic. Her army engaged in a see-saw battle with Germany across North

Africa as the Germans attempted to take Cairo and the Suez Canal. The situation seemed hopeless and the U.S. wanted to stay out of it, but that was not to be.

Relations with Japan were no better. In 1930, Japan invaded Manchuria, seeking a source of raw materials. Their total war with China began in 1937. The U.S. tried to maintain a balance of power but Japan was intent on increasing the size of her navy. The Japanese announced a Greater East Asia Co-Prosperity Sphere, intended to free the area of colonization and assure themselves a supply of raw materials for war. They were importing 80% of their oil from the U.S. and, as a counter measure, we imposed an oil embargo on Japan. One of their options was to go to war with the U.S., which they did as we were to learn the hard way.

Early in 1941 I asked my economics teacher, Mr. Grinstead, with whom I had great respect, how long he thought it would take us to win a war with Germany if we were to become involved. He estimated 10 to 15 years, considering the immense head start Germany had and our lack of preparation. I could not disagree. Actually it took 3 years and 8 months, thanks to our resolve and manufacturing capability. Russia's entry into the war on our side helped too, but the situation seemed grim at that time to say the least.

Once Japan entered the war with the U.S., all young, healthy American males would be called to serve their country. The question on my mind was whether to: (1) Get a deferment by going to work for an aircraft manufacturer. More than once while in combat, I half-thought I should have stayed home and bucked rivets for Lockheed. (2) Wait to be drafted and likely end up in the infantry. That had no appeal to me. (3) Volunteer for a branch of the service that would be interesting and educational while serving my country. I chose the latter and put my sights on pilot training.

But there was a problem. The Army Air Corps took only 20-year-olds and older. My two best friends, Wes Parlee and Brad Stewart, each of whom were 20, signed up for pilot training. I had to wait. Later, both of them washed out of pilot training school. Wes became a bombardier and endured harrowing experiences in a B-17 heavy bomber over Germany. Brad joined the Coast Guard and participated in hazardous landings in the South Pacific. Both friends survived the war, fortunately.

David with his 1934 Ford V8

David's father, Sumner M. Hayward, at his home on East Orange Grove Avenue in Pasadena

David's brother Stewart L. Hayward (Taken in 1951)

CHAPTER 3
Appointment with Destiny

ON JANUARY 24, 1942, I was flying high above the clouds, speeding eastward aboard a Western Airlines Mainliner. The trip was a strange one that I thought up on the spur of the moment and decided upon merely by a hunch.

Let's turn back the calendar a few weeks to New Year's Day 1942. My friend Wes Parlee's Uncle Ross Jenkins drove Wes, Brad Stewart, and myself to Bakersfield, California. Two events set the scene. First, it snowed heavily approaching Bakersfield for the first time in several years. Second, my two best friends, Wes and Brad, were leaving civilian life to become aviation cadets in the U.S. Army Air Corps. Originally we three planned to join at the same time but, unfortunately, as I was unable to meet the minimum age requirement of 20, our paths parted that day. Brad Stewart and Wes Parlee began their military service at Lerdo Field, Bakersfield, and I returned home to continue civilian life.

The story skips ahead two weeks to the evening of Thursday, January 15th. On that night I heard the War Department lowered the minimum age for aviation cadets to 18, so I started to move. On the next Saturday I left work a little early and changed most of my savings into defense bonds. I bought 3 bonds of $100 each, and then I told a recruiting officer my plans. He gave me an application form to take home. Before nightfall, I filled out the application in triplicate, obtained my father's signature of consent, obtained notarization of the application, and arranged for recommendation letters from Mr. Grinstead (my counselor at

Pasadena Junior College), Mr. Jacobs (stepfather of Don and Mary Lou Cobb), and Mr. Stewart (Brad's father). Having completed those things, I waited until Monday.

Sunday I took to relax. What better way than to drive to Long Beach with another friend, Julian Tucker, for one last time in the surf while still a civilian? The breakers were just as they had been all winter, small and unsuitable for good riding, but the sun was out and we enjoyed it.

Monday, returning to work, I told Stuart Leavell, my boss, about my Air Corps plans. He favored them and commented, "Dave you can do the country more good as a pilot than with the work you are doing here. You can work at Fletcher Aircraft Schools as long as you want, but let me know as soon as you have definite news of leaving." He returned my birth certificate from his file and I took it home.

I saw Sgt. Cremins, the recruiting officer, just before he closed up for the night and handed him my birth certificate and letters of recommendation. He instructed me to take my physical exam the next morning in Glendale. However, when I reported to the Air Corps Training Detachment I learned they had so many exam appointments ahead of me they had to book me for one week later.

That night I heard an Air Corps major interviewed on Bing Crosby's radio show commenting, "An applicant for the Air Corps has no choice as to whether he will be a pilot, navigator, or bombardier. It is up to the Army to decide for the applicant."

It was bad news. I reasoned that the only way to be chosen pilot would be to show the Army I was better qualified to be a pilot than either of the other two positions. Brad Stewart went into primary training immediately after enlistment, likely because he had an hour's pilot instruction beforehand. In trying for any job, preference seems to go to the man with experience. So I planned to use the week-long lull before my physical exam by getting in some flying time.

But there was a stumbling block. All civilian flying was suspended on the West Coast. I spent the night pouring over the question. The next day I called to find the nearest field where a civilian could take dual instruction. The answer was Blythe, California, over 200 miles away.

I wondered how I would get there until my friend Josie at work suggested, "Why don't you fly there?" I called the airlines only to find out that the first stop was Las Vegas, Nevada. That was miles beyond Blythe. Josie helped again by suggesting, "Go all the way to Las Vegas if it means that much to you. There must be a civilian field nearby."

I had to decide my future. Even though the trip seemed crack-pot and would cost $25 for transportation, I decided to make the trip, even though the lessons might not influence the Army at all. Soon I had reservations for the east-bound transport at 8:00 the next morning.

Aboard the airliner I was having the time of my life, observing the rugged California topography from the air. I thought, *If my hunch works, the gains will be obvious; if not, the trip will still be a marvelous adventure, although possibly lacking in common sense.*

The trip to Las Vegas was a great success although, at first, I thought it would be in vain. Upon landing in Las Vegas I saw no civilian planes at all but, after inquiring at the terminal building, I learned a flying school had just started up on the Tonopah Road on the other side of Las Vegas. So I jumped in a taxi, hurried out there, and found that Morton Air Service, formerly at Municipal Airport, Los Angeles, had just moved there the Wednesday before. So I flew for an hour, rested, and flew another hour. Flying seemed to come very easily to me and the instructor commented on how well I handled the ship.

January 27th was another important day. I took my physical exam and passed it. Of the 24 candidates who took the physical, only 14 passed. It was tough. Some men failed just because of a broken nose. Next, we were to report for an interview and written tests and, after that, go to Phoenix, Arizona for the beginning of Army life. That part turned out to be premature.

My physical exam was nothing compared to the written exam. Seven more men joined the group and 20 took the test. They gave us 150 questions, told us 75 correct was average, and then failed everyone who didn't make 90. My score was 115, and eleven of the twenty recruits passed. Two of them had to be released from the Navy and one did not have adequate application papers. No more than eight out of approximately thirty-six would be eligible to leave for Phoenix, Arizona, on the next Saturday. Some might have failed the board interview after the test.

Before Saturday arrived I received another letter from the War Department instructing me not to report for enlistment, but wait for further instructions. That presented a problem as the clothes I had on were the only ones that did not reek of moth balls; all the others were stored away. Furthermore, I had quit my job and had only $1.46 in cash. I heard the Air Corps just wasn't able to take care of the supply of volunteers, so I asked an officer, "Is it a matter of days or weeks?"

He replied, "A matter of weeks. You will have to wait for old classes to graduate and new air fields to be built."

The next letter to arrive from the War Department instructed me to report for enlistment on February 27th and leave for the Santa Ana Replacement Center on March 28th. That threw another problem my way: what to do for the next month. I wondered, *Should I go back to school, take a vacation, or what?*

I enrolled back at Pasadena Junior College thinking, *Good ole school days are here again.* The Aviation Department was run by Professor Max Harlow, an Aeronautical Engineer who designed the Harlow PJC-1 and 2, which were built there as a class project. The courses I signed up for were radio trouble shooting and maps. The map course would expose me to weather maps, topographic maps, and road maps, and should come in handy in the weeks and months to come. However, schooling only lasted one week.

On February 25th I had my first taste of what the public thought was exposure to war. The ack-ack guns down at the Los Angeles harbor opened fire for a few hours. Something was going on and the public didn't know what it was. The War Department merely called it a false alarm. Later, the *Los Angeles Times* reported, "Enemy observation planes flew over the beach cities, out of range. We lost a P-38, but it was due to engine failure. The plane went down at 3rd and Vermont." That was a busy area of Los Angeles. I heard no more about it. People seemed to have their own versions of what happened that night.

Commencing February 27, 1942, I was known as Number 19080492. Our group of candidates was inducted that day in Los Angeles. We would be given a salary of $75 per month plus a subsistence of $30 per month while at home. But we would not go to Santa Ana until March 28th. Some people in our group considered a trip to see America for the next 30 days.

*(L to R) David Hayward, Bradley Stewart
and Wesley Parlee*

The flying lesson at Las Vegas was fun.

CHAPTER 4
See America First

CADET CLYDE DINWIDDIE AND I left home on February 28th for an automobile tour around the west, with no particular itinerary in mind. He drove his 1940 Ford V-8 coupe.

In the following month Clyde and I were to follow the slogan of the time: "See America First." At our stop in Las Vegas, I lost 50 cents in the slot machines. When night came, we slept in sleeping bags in the turtle back of his car. The next day we drove by the Great Salt Lake and snow-covered Wasatch Mountains. Early the following morning, about 2:00 am, we started up the grade to the Rocky Mountains, through Red Rock Creek northwards. The scenery was exceptionally beautiful under a full moon that shone throughout the night, providing an awesome tint to the rugged mountains white with snow. In the valleys, huge snow fields completed the picture.

Then I learned of Clyde's real motive for the trip: his girlfriend lived in Anaconda, Montana. Just before dawn we arrived in Anaconda and it became our temporary base. Friends of Clyde swept us off our feet with hospitality. Clyde's girl found a friend for me so we could make it a foursome, and after nightfall we took our dates around town and had a very good time.

Clyde and I stayed in Anaconda for two weeks as guests of the Swanson family; they wouldn't let us leave. I have flashes of memory: the beautiful scenery, two main lakes frozen thick, a girl's house, playing cards, trying to be clever, June singing for us like Deanna Durbin, people being friendly and hospitable, everyone knowing everyone else, wearing skis, holding a rope, being towed down the snow-covered road behind a car, falling too many times, touring the Anaconda smelter, a snow ball battle with the kids, hitting the fun places in Anaconda, Butte, Meaderville, and points north, south, east, and west, putting in a quarter and getting back 18 quarters, nice Swedes, painting their upstairs bathroom, and dancing at the Lido with Jean. Just when I was getting to like her, an Army friend of hers showed up and she broke her date with me. But I got over it.

We found one great difference between life in Anaconda and at home. Here we spend much of our leisure riding around in automobiles or doing outdoor sports, but up there people don't go outside very often in winter time, only when they have to; their main pastime is playing pinochle. We played pinochle every day since arriving and I really got a bang out of it. They would rather play pinochle than eat. Nothing pleased Mr. Swanson more, on days when he was physically unable to work, than for Clyde and me to challenge him and his wife to a game.

More flashes of memory come to me: it snowed and snowed and snowed all day, our last big night in Butte, Club Moderne in Anaconda, Meaderville, dance halls and bars bunched together, fried chicken in Meaderville to sober everybody up, to bed by 3:30 am, washing the kitchen walls and ceiling, spectacular winter scenes in Deerlodge National Forest, and people fishing through holes in the ice.

Sadly, Clyde and I said goodbye to them. Mrs. Swanson sent us on our way with a big lunch to take with us. We stopped at a florist and had an arrangement made for them at a cost of $2.00.

Clyde and I still had 10 days left before reporting to Santa Ana. We headed home via the Columbia River, Portland, Eugene, Crescent City, Redwood Highway, Golden Gate, Tulare (where we stopped to see Wes Parlee, just finishing his primary flight training), and arrived home March 20th, broke and nearly out of gas.

My automobile tour of the American west with Clyde was a wonderful experience. Clyde became engaged to the Swanson girl. He was my roommate at Santa Ana and made it through flight training, advanced to the P-38 fighter plane, and was assigned to combat duty in North Africa. The rest of the story is very sad. On May 12, 1943, Clyde was killed while flying his P-38 at Oran, North Africa. I was saddened to lose a good friend. Unfortunately, a footnote such as this would be common in future months.

With six days left before reporting to Santa Ana, I still had time to catch up on my sleep, drive my Ford V-8, visit the Walters girls (one of them was the girlfriend of my good friend Chuck O'Hara), swim with friends at Long Beach, go to movies, visit again with the gang at Fletcher Aviation, win 25 cents at poker, and close up my affairs for the next phase of my life.

Dave Hayward and Clyde Dinwiddie in Anaconda, Montana

This was fun and there was plenty of snow.

CHAPTER 5
Encountering Ack Ack

MY SECOND COMBAT MISSION began just nine days after the first one, April 17, 1943. Our squadron flew to the heavily defended Myitnge Bridge (pronounced My Tinj), crossing a tributary to the Irrawaddy River near Mandalay, Burma. The overall assignment of the 341st Bomb Group, of which the 22nd Bomb Squadron was a part, was to destroy Japanese capability to move troops and supplies into northern Burma. Rangoon and Mandalay fell in 1942. Japan invaded India and threatened to cut off all supplies to China. The Myitnge Bridge was vital to the Japanese supply line. It was well protected, as was the city of Mandalay, with the heaviest anti-aircraft fire we were to see.

That mission was nearly as bad as the first. As we entered the bombing run, black puffs of smoke appeared ahead. The pilot could not alter his altitude or air speed, as it would interfere with the bombardier's aim. We could only fly straight ahead, into the black puffs, grit our teeth, and hope for the best.

When an anti-aircraft shell goes off under an airplane, the crew feels a sharp buffeting and hears what sounds like buckshot being fired against a metal building. This was happening and it was scary. One of my favorite cartoons appeared in a wartime military publication showing a British sergeant standing next to his anti-aircraft gun as an officer approached and asked, "I say there, sergeant, have you shot down any planes today?"

The sergeant replied, "No Sir, I have not, but I think I scared one or two rather badly."

The message stuck with me. News media were quick to point out how many planes were shot down on a given mission but seldom did they comment on how many airmen were scared "rather badly" in the process. It was a burden the air crews had to bear.

As it turned out, all our aircraft made it back to the base that day. However, we had a few holes in our plane, as did many of the others. On later missions, some of our planes and crews did not survive those black puffs.

For every plane shot down by anti-aircraft fire there were numerous incidents of close calls where the plane could easily have been shot down except for the Grace of God. One example is described by Jay Percival, the cannoneer-navigator aboard Wendell Hanson's plane on a raid on Japanese aircraft parked on the ground at the airport at Chiang Mai, Thailand. Jay was flying in a B-25 H model which was equipped with a 75 mm cannon in the nose. It was Jay's job to load the cannon so it could be fired by the pilot. Jay reported:

> We got hit with a 20 mm anti-aircraft shell that ruptured the hydraulic system. It also came through the back of the aluminum cannoneer's seat where I had been sitting. The only reason I wasn't hit was that I was standing to take another 75 mm shell out of the rack to reload the cannon. It was then that I noticed the pink hydraulic fluid on the floor where I was standing.

It was amazing how much punishment a B-25 could take, as it had relatively few vulnerable places. Armor plate was installed under the pilots' seats. Gasoline tanks were self-sealing. Engines were air-cooled, compact radials with no complex liquid cooling system. Whatever our B-25s may have given up in speed we gained in safety.

Headquarters staff had the problem of evaluating the cost of those missions in terms of airmen and aircraft lost versus the effectiveness of our attacks on enemy installations. Pilots tried to determine the degree of success as soon as possible, but sitting in the pilot's compartment up front, we could not easily observe whether our bombs hit the intended target. Sometimes a crew member seated in the back of the plane could see the results and would report to those up front.

The best way to evaluate our effectiveness was by aerial photography, analyzed back at the base. One of my photos, taken of the Myitnge Bridge, shows two spans, one for rail traffic and the other for motor vehicles. One span was taken out previously and on the other span our bombs hit one end of the bridge, thereby accomplishing the mission's purpose for that day.

I did not go back to the Myitnge Bridge. Either it was sufficiently knocked out for the time being or our planners reasoned that, because of the heavy concentration of flak, sending in medium bombers at 12,000 feet altitude was not a good tactic. B-24 heavy bombers could fly over at a higher, safer altitude and do the job.

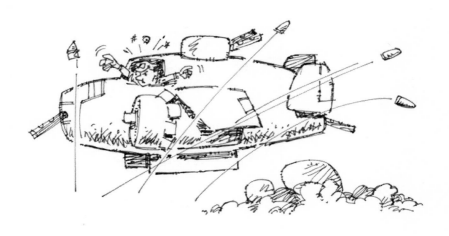

C'mon, fellas! Take it easy!

CHAPTER 6
At Santa Ana

ONLY SIX MILES TO the south was Balboa where the boys back home were whooping it up that Easter week, so near and yet so far. Soon after arrival in camp our cadets received coveralls and blankets and, almost immediately, were assigned to KP (kitchen police) duty. It lasted all day and into the night.

Santa Ana Replacement Center in California, later known as Santa Ana Army Air Base, was located on what is now Orange County Fair Grounds and Orange Coast College. The first group of cadets arrived in February 1942. We were the second group, Class 42-J, arriving March 27, 1942, and remained for one month before going on to Primary Flying School.

The base planned to offer ground school classes for cadets before entering their flight training, to provide knowledge in navigation, communications, weather, armament, etc. Unfortunately, we arrived too soon for that feature and had little or no ground school, nor paved roads either. Making it worse, the month of April was an exceptionally rainy month.

But Santa Ana did provide cadets with uniforms and rifles and they gave us the shots we needed for typhoid, tetanus, and yellow fever, along with what seemed like endless physical exams. To keep men busy and out of trouble they marched us for what seemed like hours every day. The marching music of John Phillips Sousa came booming over loud speakers and was stirring to hear, but most of it got monotonous after a while. My recollection of Santa Ana is still dominated by endless marching through mud while my arms ached with the shots they gave us.

On the day after arrival we were awakened at 4:30 am and put on KP duty which went on for 36 hours. Typical duties were washing dishes and peeling potatoes. I soon learned how to "gold brick," that is, do as little of that as I could get away with.

Two days later we marched continually for three hours, by companies. Short men marched in the front of the line and the tallest (me) in the rear. Front men took large steps while rear men took shorter ones. We listened carefully to the shouts of the platoon commander, "Column left, march!" Then, "Column right…mark time…present arms…about face." Every so often the commander shouted, "Cut down that arm swing, misters!" or "Count cadence, count!" Our response was, "Hut, two, three, four, hut, two, three, four," and so on.

The good part was the Army broke me of a bad habit I had as a teenager, of rolling onto the ball of my foot and rising with each step. It was not permitted in the Army. The really bad part was when it rained. Roads were not yet paved and the adobe soil became very sticky in the rain. I sunk into the mud all the way to my ankles. Sometimes when I stepped forward my feet pulled out of my shoes, leaving them behind. What a mess that was to clean up! The army's purpose of marching, we were told, was to establish discipline, but I was convinced it was to keep us busy while the authorities had nothing else for us to do.

We cadets took more exams, physical to determine depth perception, and written to determine whether we would go to pilot training, bombardier, or navigator school. In one of our tests we put pegs in holes; I wasn't quite sure what that was supposed to accomplish.

One of our responsibilities was to draw guard duty. My post was the enlisted men's barracks from 11 pm to 3 am. When walking in the mud in the rain, my rifle seemed impossibly heavy. They gave cadets athletic training: chin-ups, leg-lifts, push-ups, and pull-ups. I did the 75 yard dash in 9.5 seconds and the 150 yard dash in 19.8 seconds. Then they gave us instruction in the use of gas masks. After that, the medical corps put us in a huge steel cylinder, evacuated half of the air, and "took us up" to 15,000 feet equivalent to test us for high altitude endurance. Later we went to the equivalent of 40,000 feet, that time using oxygen.

Cadets had some contact with the outside. On April 9th I learned about the fall of Bataan in the Philippines. A good friend of mine, Jack Donnelly, was there. Someone at home sent me a newspaper article reporting, "John (Jack) Donnelly was severely wounded in action in the Philippine Islands on January 7." Later I received the sad news that he died on the Bataan death march. I lost another good friend.

On the lighter side, my brother Stewart came to visit. He had applied to enter the U.S. Navy and was working for Lockheed Aircraft while waiting to be accepted. Stew, as we called him, brought with him a very nice lady, Alice Storey, whom he married in November of that year. I gave Stew my civilian clothes and asked him to take them home.

Morale picked up on the day we marched in a parade. To add to the drama, a P-38 fighter plane dove over the parade ground to thrill the crowd. Morale improved even more when Hollywood entertainers visited: Edgar Bergen, Charlie McCarthy, Jeanette McDonald, and Ray Noble and his orchestra. Abbott and Costello also put on a show.

From time to time the base issued passes to cadets. The first such time, 100 passes were handed out but I was in the shower and missed getting one.

On April 18th my pal Brad Stewart came over to my barrack. He was at Santa Ana awaiting further assignment, bearing sad news that he washed out of pilot training. Brad and I hitchhiked into Hollywood. At the Hollywood Roosevelt Hotel we met two other cadets, had dinner, stopped at Streets of Paris, went roller skating at the Roller Bowl, bowled a line, and returned to Brad's parent's house in Los Angeles for a good night's sleep and hearty breakfast the next morning.

Unknown to me at that time, April 18th was the day the Doolittle raiders attacked Japan with their B-25s from the aircraft carrier USS Hornet. It was a bold, reassuring raid. I would know some of the participants later.

On April 23rd we turned in our bedding, sat around until after evening mess, climbed into GI trucks, rode to the railroad station, and boarded Pullman cars. I was glad to move to Primary Flying School, but I wrote at the time, "I now have the worst cold of my life and really feel bad. Let's hope the morning will bring relief."

After the war, although the Santa Ana Army Air Base was turned into a fair ground and a college, veterans who served there in World War II continued to have annual reunions at the college. Their group was known as the Santa Ana Army Air Base Wing. I attended many of the reunions. They also maintain a museum of World War II memorabilia; I donated my Air Force uniform to the museum.

Marching in the sticky mud

*The Army
gave the
cadets shots
of all kinds.*

*Dave Hayward
shows off his new
coveralls and
flight cap.*

CHAPTER 7
Boondoggle Over Tibet

THE UPPER BRAHMAPUTRA RIVER wound its way into the majestic mountains of eastern Tibet. What scenery! From our flying altitude of 20,000 feet it looked like Yosemite Valley but many times larger, a perfectly glaciated valley with steep sides, hanging tributaries, and a meandering river in the flat valley floor below. My geology teacher back at Pasadena Junior College would envy my experience.

Let me explain. As I left Santa Ana and headed for Primary Flying School aboard that Pullman car, I had lots of time to think, wondering what the future might bring. I'd probably be going to a war zone and fly a military aircraft. Beyond that, who knows? Not in my wildest dreams would I have imagined the day of May 2, 1943.

Lt. Patrick Ham parked our B-25 medium bomber alongside the airfield at Dinjan, in Assam Province, the most northeastern part of India. It was after my third combat mission and I was still in my indoctrination period of flying as copilot for an experienced pilot, this time Pat Ham.

A colonel walked up to Pat and told him, "I get reports that a Japanese homing station is somewhere in these mountains." He pointed westward toward Tibet and continued, "Our pilots complain the Japanese are luring our cargo planes off course. I want to locate that station, but I need your B-25. With its twin engines and radio compass I should have a good chance of finding it."

The colonel asked Pat if he would go along but "No thank you, Sir," was Pat's reply. Next, the colonel asked me and I accepted, so off we went. I was the colonel's copilot that day.

At 10,000 feet the colonel and I donned our oxygen masks and I engaged the superchargers. We climbed to 20,000 feet, flying westerly into the valley. Mountains on either side reached up to our altitude and rose even higher ahead to 29,029 feet at Mt. Everest. Native settlements hung on the valley walls, with rows of primitive crops growing where the slopes would allow. I brought my camera along to preserve some of those images.

Soon the valley we were flying through narrowed as it turned north. The B-25 could not climb much higher, so we turned around while we could do so safely. At 20,000 feet the colonel was careful to avoid a high altitude stall, making his turn slowly. I wondered, *What would we do if an engine failed up here? Make an emergency landing on the valley floor? But who would find us? Besides, Tibet is a neutral country. We are not supposed to be here in the first place. We could be interned for the rest of the war.*

The B-25 performed faithfully and we made it back to Dinjan for a total of 2 hours and 30 minutes of flight time. That night the ten people aboard our flight talked over the day's experience. While there may have been some truth to reports of a Japanese homing station luring our cargo planes off course, I wondered if the colonel really planned the day as just a good opportunity to take his friends on a sight-seeing trip to view spectacular scenery they would never see again.

Our airplane was designed for six persons, with only six oxygen outlets. The colonel and I were well provided for but the other eight people had to share four oxygen masks. I was not surprised when some of them complained of splitting headaches that night.

As a footnote, I did not get credit for a combat mission that day. It might be argued that we were on a "search and destroy" mission looking for an enemy installation which, if found, we would destroy. Technically, we were not flying over enemy territory, and that usually determined whether it was a combat mission; we carried no bombs. But I wondered, *Could the person who determined whether it was a combat mission have been as skeptical as I was? We found no enemy homing station and did not even turn on our radio compass to look for one.*

As a second footnote, after the war we learned that the Japanese actually did have a radio station that broadcast false signals to lure American cargo aircraft off course so they would fly into mountainsides. But the station was not located in the scenic mountains of Tibet. It was in the jungle near the village of Sumprabum in northern Burma, 100 miles south of the nearest border with Tibet and nearly 300 miles southeast of the area where we were enjoying the scenery that day. Our flight was truly a boondoggle.

The B-25 had twin engines and a radio compass which made it ideal for the intended mission.

The Himalaya Mountains of Tibet, photographed by David Hayward from the window of his B-25.

The valley narrowed and turned to the north. It was time to turn around while still possible.

CHAPTER 8
The Wild Blue Yonder

IN THE YEAR 1938, Robert Crawford wrote "The Air Force Song," of which the opening lines are:

Off we go into the wild blue yonder,
Climbing high into the sky.

That's the way Class 42-J felt on Saturday, April 25, 1942, as we arrived at the Rankin Aeronautical Academy in Tulare, California, for Primary Flight School training. Tulare is in San Joaquin Valley, 165 miles north of Los Angeles. Our purpose was to fly the Stearman PT-17 biplane, known for its ability with acrobatic maneuvers.

The rooms and mess hall were wonderful at Tulare, compared with our facility at Santa Ana. I found the hospital, as my cold was still bad and my right ear painful. They "fixed it up," according to my diary.

The cadets attended a lecture on conduct and then met our flight instructors. Mine was Mr. D. L. Chapman, a civilian whom I found to be very helpful. Five cadets were assigned to him. He taught us what an aileron is and how to use a parachute. The next day he took me up for 35 minutes of flying time, doing just straight and level flight. I was impressed; the Stearmans were fine airplanes, sturdy and large, responsive to the controls and heavier than a Piper Cub. Consequently, they did not bounce around as much as a Piper would. My flight instruction at Las

39

Vegas might have helped, as Mr. Chapman seemed to leave so much up to me.

Inevitably, I learned what a nuisance an upperclassman could be, as they pestered us continually, leaving only 9:30 to 10:00 pm for ourselves. The upperclassmen's weekend passes were cancelled because the rooms of us "dodos" were not neat enough. That sounded like trouble (Dodos were extinct birds that could not fly, a term applied to underclassmen).

On a day of rain we stayed in our rooms and studied. Unfortunately, that gave the upperclassmen a chance to harass us. One of my roommates loved to wise crack and tried to counter the hazing by talking back with witty remarks. The upperclassmen laid for him and broke down his spirits until he almost cried, which was pathetic to witness.

Mr. Chapman conquered any fear of air sickness, as he showed me a spin, some power stalls, a couple of simulated forced landings, and a landing, all without any ill effects by me. I felt enthusiastic about flying.

One day Mr. Chapman gave all his students "pink slips" (failing grades). Was it just a trick to knock out any overconfidence? Maybe. After that, he and I went back to flying and did a wing over and dove at full throttle towards the ground, reaching a velocity of 250 mph. The plane was not supposed to be flown faster than 186 mph, but the Stearman showed no signs of strain.

Our first Sunday was a no-fly day. Some men left on open post. Others walked punishment tours or were stuck with duties. Bob Hamilton, one of my roommates, brought back his airplane late. His instructor made him salute the clock every 30 seconds for a half hour. No open post for him! I was on guard duty all night, 2 hours on and 4 hours off, plodding around the large north hangar and carrying a 12 gauge, double-barreled shotgun. The 2 hours seemed like a day and the 4 hours off like 5 minutes.

On two successive days nearly all of our five students got pink slips, which could mean check rides. That worried me, as I liked flying very much, was crazy about it, and felt I had the ability to continue. It was reassuring the next day when Mr. Chapman told me, "You have improved 100%. There will be no pink slip." I was relieved but wondered, *Could he have another motive? If he gave too many pink slips, resulting in check rides, that could lead to a change of instructors and he wouldn't want to lose all his students. Mr. Chapman might have been playing games with us, just trying to get the best possible effort out of us.*

One Saturday night three cadets came in after hours and refused to identify themselves. "Brace" Bradley, the captain, announced he would confine everybody on all weekends unless those three cadets gave themselves up. Captain Bradley was noted for approaching a cadet and ordering, "All right, mister, hit a brace!" A "brace" was a position of rigid attention, with the small of the back pressed firmly against a wall. Thus, he gained the nickname. But some of the "washed out" cadets were to leave for Santa Ana by the weekend and could not be present for the punishment. So "Brace" Bradley ordered them to walk their punishment tours all evening. Either the after-hours cadets or "Brace" Bradley gave in, because we did return to open post on the following Saturday night.

Captain Bradley called all "dodos" out to the parade ground one day and put us in a "brace" for a whole hour while he insulted and threatened us. The battalion was busy afterward diagnosing him. Was he suffering from an inferiority complex and felt he had to take it out on us?

May 12th was my 20th birthday, highlighted by receiving a letter from my brother Stewart who told me he was about to be married to his girlfriend, Alice. I was happy for him.

On May 14th I soloed! What a thrill! It seemed great to be the master of the ship. The next day Mr. Chapman was absent, so the flight commander took over. He gave me some good criticism but also pointed out, "Sometimes you fly just well enough to get there. I want you to strive for perfection." That gave me something to work on.

Saturdays and Sundays, when cadets had no flying, we attended ground school and had personal inspections and battalion reviews on certain days. Upperclassmen usually conducted the personal inspections, passing through our rooms wearing white gloves and feeling for dust, seeing that our shoes were polished and that sort of thing. Any violations resulted in punishment tours.

The battalion reviews required our standing at parade rest or attention for one hour. If anyone fainted he would be in trouble. Those were hot summer days in the San Joaquin Valley, but no cadet passed out. Another time we stood at attention for over 2 hours, learning very quickly that by flexing our knees slightly, blood would continue to circulate in our legs and we would be less likely to faint.

On open post days I did very little, sometimes just escaping to an inexpensive movie in town. Some cadets swam in a pool in Tulare and others drove up to Sequoia National Park not far away.

Jim Hamer, one of my roommates, became my best friend as time went on. He was what we called a "hot pilot," meaning a very aggressive pilot. However, he "ground looped," which means he caught a wing tip on the ground while landing, causing the plane to spin around and result in some damage. He did that twice in one day and was sent for a check ride. Fortunately, Jim passed it and continued with the program. He was a good looking, outgoing, expressive sort of guy, with a perpetual smile on his face. The girls were crazy about him.

One day I gave Mr. Chapman a good ride so he sent me up for more solo time. He and I came to an understanding and he noted, "I finally found out what is the matter with you, an inferiority complex. You are not aggressive enough. We'll work on that and conquer it."

Later, when I was overseas flying in combat, I learned that all pilots, whether fighter or bomber pilots, had to know where to draw the line between aggression and caution. Bomber pilots were responsible for a crew of five or more along with an expensive airplane that someone had to bring halfway around the world to meet the enemy. Little was gained by showing off as a "hot pilot." Unfortunately, in combat our low-level missions required a higher degree of aggressiveness and we did take casualties as a result. But it seemed a disproportionate number of our "hot pilots" did not return home.

One of my classmates, Cadet Carl Larson, died when he was doing figure S's along a road and his plane spun to the ground, burning on impact. He was a likeable fellow and it was a shock and shame to lose him. Under those circumstances, the family normally would receive an official letter from the government expressing regret, along with a $10,000 life insurance payment. If possible, a member of the military would accompany the casket to the family. The Stearman airplane could be replaced for $14,000.

On the upperclassmen's graduation day I was confined for "gigs" and given the job of CQ (Charge of Quarters). That meant staying up until 3 am. I still had to walk five hours of punishment tours the next day. Just before the upperclassmen left they rolled over our beds with us in them. Then they went into town to get into "good spirits." After that, the rules were changed prohibiting any hazing, lack of privileges, or special duties for dodos. The timing of that rule change was disappointing for us cadets who were about to become upperclassmen ourselves.

The Stearman PT-17 primary training plane

Roommate Bob Hamilton returned his airplane late and had to salute the clock every 30 seconds for half an hour.

Back row: Dave Hayward is in the center.
Jim Hamer is on the right end.

The Army issued cadets a leather jacket…

…and a scarf and goggles.

CHAPTER 9
No Longer a Dodo

SOMETIMES I WONDERED ABOUT the new dodos. They certainly didn't act like officers yet, and if we couldn't use severe disciplinary measures anymore, I felt they probably would never learn the correct ways to do things. They did not speak with proper respect, their rooms were not neat, and other things were quite noticeable. All we could do was tell them right from wrong and just hope it would sink in.

By the beginning of our second month I was doing solo spins and had the confident feeling that it was only me who could bring that plane out of a spin. At that time about 30% of the cadets were washed out and sent back to Santa Ana for reassignment. My instructor showed me some chandelles and lazy eights, the beginning of acrobatics. I resolved from then on I would fly the airplane instead of letting it fly me.

One day we learned some Japanese had escaped from a concentration camp in Tulare. Cadets were put on alert, with an air raid drill and gas masks. The mechanics spread our airplanes all over the field. Our guard was tripled and equipped with side arms and no open post was permitted. However, we had no follow-up news to the incident.

Every morning when a typical cadet awoke he felt like saying, "Well, it's only 16 hours until I can go back to bed. That won't be so bad." Right after breakfast, while we watched a motion picture on a ground school subject, most of the class probably got a little shut-eye. That was followed by athletics and ground school again, a possible time for more rest. Then came dinner and after that we would go to the flight line. Cadets learned to sleep any time they were not in an airplane.

On June 5th one of the C Company dodos went up without fastening his safety belt. His instructor showed him a spin and, in doing so, the dodo fell out of the plane. When he regained his senses he grabbed madly at the shoulder strap of his parachute. After noticing he did not have the ring in his hand, he located it and yanked the ring so hard it pulled completely out of the rigging. He thought he had broken the mechanism. But after a while he felt a jarring about his shoulders and floated down. In landing, he turned his ankle. He washed out.

Pay days were happy days. According to one entry, I received $141.40 for one month, but they took away $65 for board and room and another $5 for miscellaneous items. Even so, money was piling up faster than I could spend it. There just wasn't much to spend it on. My main expense was for Cokes between ground school classes. I had about $165 on hand and planned to send almost half of it home.

Melvin Heflinger was a good friend whom I had grown up with. Before the war, we hiked the San Gabriel Mountains together, just Mel, his father, his dog, and me. I spent a lot of time with the Heflinger family. They were very good to me. Mel took private flying lessons before the war and ended up as one of the instructors at Tulare, quite a coincidence. I was curious as to any comments Mr. Chapman might have said to him. Mel replied, "Dave, you don't want to hear this, but last time I talked to your instructor was the day you ground looped, and he was so mad that his opinion of you was definitely one-sided."

Every night after supper we had a bull session in our room. On one occasion the fellows were debating the point of shooting an enemy flier while parachuting. My comment was, "It's interesting to argue, but none of us would really know what we would do until we actually experienced it. Conceivably in a fit of anger a pilot would lose his senses temporarily and do something like that. I can't picture it myself, though."

On June 10th we had a follow-up to the "Brace" Bradley story. Something very strange happened to our commandant of cadets. He came down off his high horse and complimented us on the way we were marching lately. Then he revoked his previous order for us to get to all formations five minutes early. To top it off, he gave open post every Wednesday night to all men with ground school grades of 85% or above. I was eligible, but there wasn't much to do in town on a week night, so I stayed at the base.

The 60 hour check ride was the next big thing facing us cadets. Mr. Chapman said the lieutenant would look mainly for two things: good coordination and safety. So I went up and practiced my acrobatics solo, which went OK except that in my slow roll, I dropped my nose, so I decided to end the maneuver as a split-S. I gave myself a check ride, pretending the lieutenant was sitting up there in the front seat. During the hour and a quarter I did everything I was taught to do and afterward felt very well and confident, so I went up on the check ride and passed it OK. The only thing I did that griped the lieutenant was that I forgot to salute him and be formally dismissed. But he got over it and so did I. The climax was over.

On June 13th I had a 24 hour pass. It cost me $5 for someone to take my place doing punishment tours at Rankin, $1 for the bus ride, $7 for the plane ride, and $1.50 for the taxi home. The next morning in Pasadena I was awakened at 6:30 am by my brother Stewart and my father. Stewart was still waiting to be accepted by the Navy. My father was not feeling well, showing signs of depression and confusion, although he was fully able to take care of himself. But as time went on his condition worsened and he suffered a series of strokes. He lived through the war years and continued until 1947; he saw his two sons return safely from the war and was able to spend time with his granddaughter, Sandra. My brother and I did our best to look after dad, as difficult as it was with the war going on.

During my 24-hour pass I tried to catch up with my friends. Wes Parlee washed out of pilot training school at Luke Field, Arizona. Some of my friends married: Mary Lou Cobb and a soldier from Texas, Chuck O'Hara and Pat Walters, Don Cobb and Norma Landeck, and Novia Greene and Mort Simpson.

About 3 pm I jumped in my Ford V-8, picked up Jim Hamer in Eagle Rock, and headed back to Tulare. We continued training with cross-country flights, such as to Corcoran where our flight landed and took off again for Lost Hills. Jim Hamer got lost and flew as far as Bakersfield. From Lost Hills we flew to Porterville and then returned to Rankin at Tulare.

Mr. Chapman told me to practice acrobatics. I finally caught on to doing slow rolls. The idea was to coordinate smoothly and keep the nose above the horizon. During that flight I noticed a Hudson bomber flying south, so I spiraled upward, whipped into a vertical turn and swooped down on him. He was in my sights for a good half minute. I dove down from above and followed him for quite a way. That was fun. I now had 54 hours and 56 minutes of flight time in the Stearman.

Something I did might have been a dirty trick, but was not intended that way. I practiced acrobatics until I had them down pat, and then I flew over the Japanese concentration camp to show them what beautiful slow rolls and Immelmann turns (a type of acrobatics) we American pilots could do. I wasn't intentionally trying to rub it in, but figured it gave them something to watch. In hindsight, it wasn't the right thing to do.

Mr. Chapman took me up for one last time at Rankin and did all sorts of screwball things while flying the plane. After we landed he said to me, angrily, "I killed you three times. You shouldn't have let me get away with it. You should have been on the controls right away." But he was having such a fine time I did nothing to stop it. After the flight, we climbed out and he said, "Well, Hayward, you're through flying at Rankin." Three of his original five students survived primary training. I was one of them, having completed the 60 hours required for Primary Flying School.

One last open post awaited us at Rankin. I paid a dodo to walk my punishment tour and then headed down Highway 99 toward Pasadena. I stopped to see the Walters girls, enjoyed a nice barbeque dinner, and then went to a movie. Going home was becoming depressing. Most of the girls were getting married, all the boys were gone, and the ego which I unconsciously developed caused me to talk mostly about flying, which the folks back home didn't care too much about. But the next morning I saw Wes Parlee on his way for reassignment at Santa Ana. Brad Stewart was in town, too; he had been in the Coast Guard for two days. I never expected the three of us would get together again so soon.

Back at Rankin, it was a day of leisure for us upperclassmen. None of us bothered to make the reveille formation and only a few made it to breakfast. The rest of the day was for "bunk fatigue." In the evening I attended a banquet for the graduating class. Tex Rankin, after whom the base was named, gave us all cocktails and then served us a steak dinner, all we could eat. Mr. Chapman was there. He really went for those steaks. That's when he told me, "I gave you a 'very satisfactory' for your final flying grade." I thanked him and told him what a pleasure it was to have worked with him.

The next day, Jim Hamer and I left Tulare in my Ford V-8 on our way to our next assignment at Lemoore, about 25 miles west of Tulare. On the way, I got a bright idea. "Instead of staying at a hotel in Fresno why not drive up to Sequoia National Park? It's only about 50 miles away in the Sierra Nevada Mountains?" I suggested. So that's what we did and found Sequoia to be a quiet, restful place, neither glamorous nor flashy as expected. We attended the campfire, had a very good night's sleep among the tall redwoods, were awakened the next morning by the Park management, as requested, and then proceeded down the mountain on our way to Lemoore.

Walking punishment tours

Bunk fatigue was popular with the cadets. Dave agreed.

Wes Parlee (left) was headed for reassignment.

*A dodo fell out of a
plane and grabbed
madly at the shoulder
strap of his parachute.
He washed out.*

CHAPTER 10
Wendell Hanson

WENDELL AND I FOLLOWED each other from base to base, starting with Santa Ana. Recently he said to me, "Dave, we were twins." If so, he was born first. He had the jump on most of Class 42-J because of his earlier service in the Army Air Corps. Wendell enlisted September 17, 1941, after attending college at University of Texas, and went to Missouri for basic training in the Army. When it came time for assignment he chose pilot training and arrived at Santa Ana in January 1942. Whether due to previous service or his innate leadership qualities, the commandant at Tulare appointed him platoon commander which meant, among other things, he was in charge of marching the cadets. When I say Wendell had leadership qualities I mean he was tall and dominant, had a clear and direct way of speaking, would look you directly in the eye, wore a winsome smile, and was quite convincing in making his arguments.

We trained at the same bases, graduated together, rode the same passenger plane to India, served in India and China together, flew on some of the same combat missions, completed those missions within one day of each other, returned to the U.S. on the same plane, and reported to Santa Monica for reassignment at the same time.

One day at Tulare, while Wendell was leading the cadets in a marching drill, he came to the point when he shouted "Halt." Just then an apple flew through the air and hit him just below the skull, knocking him "silly," as he described it. He sat down on some steps and the first thing he saw when he regained his senses was a group of 50 or 60 cadets standing over him, wanting to help. Wendell picked up the apple and called out, "One of you cadets threw this apple at me. Don't you know you could be washing dishes for this? I want to know who did this."

After an awkward delay a cadet in the back row replied, "I did it. What do you want me to do? Go out back and fight it out?"

Wendell countered with, "How long have you been in the service, mister? About five minutes? Any time you hit the commanding officer you are subject to a courts martial. Now get back in line." Wendell told me the incident taught him a whole lot about leadership that was valuable to him in the future.

Later, when we were training with the B-25 medium bomber at Greenville, South Carolina, one of our crews had a most unfortunate accident. The plane in which they were flying exploded in mid-air and the entire crew was lost. Just three days before the accident I had soloed with the pilot, Lt. Herbert Barton. I was shocked, of course.

Wendell walked into my room and said to me, "Dave, the captain ordered you and me to identify the bodies." So I jumped in the car waiting outside and together we went to the morgue for our very unpleasant task. It was gruesome indeed and brought home the realization that something similar could happen to any of us if our foresight and luck did not hold out. Months later, Wendell sheepishly admitted, "Dave, I have to confess that the captain ordered just me to go to the morgue and identify the bodies. I asked you because you are a friend and I needed your support." *That rascal!* I thought.

Even so, Wendell remained one of my best friends. Years later I asked him, "Do you remember my going with you to the morgue?"

He replied, "Not that part of it. The whole thing was so gruesome I tried to put it out of my mind."

The captain had further orders for Wendell Hanson, to accompany the remains of Lt. Barton to his family in Texas, which he did. As Wendell was leaving for return to Greenville, one of the Barton family members approached him carrying a little Cocker Spaniel puppy and said, "Lieutenant, we appreciate your coming to Texas at this unpleasant time. As a token of our thanks, would you accept this little puppy?"

Wendell didn't know quite what to say. What could he say except, "Yes, thank you, I will be happy to show this cute little guy to my friends back in Greenville?"

When Wendell arrived in Greenville with his dog "Taffy" it was Christmas time and a group of us were preparing a party for some poor kids who lived near the base. Wendell picked up his little Cocker Spaniel and rode with us into town. More than one shopper stopped to admire the beautiful Taffy. Wendell told me later his plan, "I am going to give Taffy a physical exam in a day or two and send him to ground school for four weeks and then check him out in a B-25."

As we left to go overseas, Wendell smuggled the little dog, whose name was "Captain Taffy" by then, aboard our transport plane and brought him through the Caribbean, across South America, the South Atlantic Ocean, Africa, around Arabia, and into India. There at Agra, site of the famous Taj Mahal, Taffy missed our plane. After all that effort and loving attachment, poor Wendell's heart was broken. But, who knows, perhaps some little boy in Karachi or Agra, India, gained a new friend.

On Wendell's 50th and final combat mission he led a daring nine-plane raid on the Japanese-held airfield at Chiang Mai, Thailand. The mission was highly successful in that they destroyed a number of enemy planes on the ground just as the Japanese were planning an air raid against friendly territory. With luck and stamina on their side, his flight accomplished what they set out to do.

But Wendell's plane was hit by a 20 mm anti-aircraft shell that knocked out his hydraulic system, causing him to crash land at Kunming. The 491st Bomb Squadron, also based at Yangkai, contributed three of the nine airplanes that day. One of their planes failed to return. Wendell and all those who returned were exhausted, both physically and emotionally, after their long 6-hour flight. As he emerged from the top hatch of his wrecked B-25 airplane, he said to himself, "I think my luck has run out."

In October 1991, thirty veterans of the 22nd Bomb Squadron along with 35 family members and friends met for their annual reunion in Kansas City, Missouri. Wendell and his wife Helen were among them. Kansas City was important to the 22nd Bomb Squadron because two-thirds of the 9,868 North American Aviation B-25s were made there. Two of the Doolittle raiders, Colonels Bill Bower and Travis Hoover, flew in to join the group with a beautifully restored B-25. Local news media covered the event and we found ourselves on TV.

Toward the end of the meeting, President Norman Sloan asked, "Where shall we meet next year? Is anyone willing to put on a reunion?"

Wendell Hanson raised his hand, "Come to the Black Hills of South Dakota. I'll show you a reunion you won't forget."

Sure enough, the reunion of 1992 was truly outstanding. Wendell took us to Ellsworth Air force Base, home of the B-1 bombers, and then to the Homestake gold mine, and the mining town of Deadwood. We viewed the Mount Rushmore Memorial and the on-going sculpture at Crazy Horse Mountain. At Black Hills National Cemetery we held our annual ceremony to honor fallen comrades.

No reunion would be complete without the enjoyment of seeing old friends and trading stories. I was particularly pleased to get together again with Loyal G. "LG" Brown, with whom I flew my first mission. Also, I met again with Pat Ham, the pilot who flew with me on a series of single-plane missions that we volunteered for soon after my arrival in India. Two other close friends from India were there as well: Wayne Craven and Jim Sullivan, both of whom lived in my basha in India. How great it was to see them again after all those years.

Wendell Hanson played an important role in the reunion held in Tucson, Arizona, in 2001. Twenty four veterans attended in a group of sixty three registrants. Wendell's navigator on the Chiang Mai raid, Jay Percival, was there too, along with his son Wayne. The Percivals presented a painting created by Wayne, depicting B-25s attacking that enemy airfield at Chiang Mai. A copy of the picture hangs on my office wall today. Together, Wendell and Jay presented a copy to the PIMA Air and Space Museum in Tucson, where much of the memorabilia of the 22nd Bomb Squadron is stored and on display.

Another important veteran joined us at Tucson, John A. Johns. Not only was John a participating pilot in the Chiang Mai raid, but he became nationally known as a caricaturist. I worked closely with John over the years as he prepared illustrations and advised on the design of our 22nd Bomb Squadron publications. The PIMA Museum put on a special display of John's work while we were in Tucson.

Wendell and his puppy "Captain Taffy" at Greenville

The Black Hills, South Dakota, reunion. Left to right: Dave Hayward, Wendell Hanson and Pat Ham

*Left to right: Jim Schooley, Wendell Hanson
and Dave Hayward*

*On Wendell's last combat mission, he led a flight of B-25s to the
Chiang Mai, Thailand, airfield and caught enemy aircraft on the
ground.*

CHAPTER 11
Basic Flying School

LEMOORE AIR BASE, VENUE for our Basic Flying School in California, gave the feel of a real Army base—similar to Santa Ana, but a contrast to the Rankin Academy and its country club atmosphere. The food was not as good and our processing period consisted of marching, lecture, marching, and lecture, repeated all day long. Marching cadence was stepped up to 180 per minute, causing the cadets to nearly pass out by nightfall. Any offense such as wandering out of bounds on weekends was grounds for elimination.

Next day was better. The Hanford Bachelorettes, a women's club, threw a barbeque for our class in nearby Hanford. Although cadets outnumbered the girls five to one, we all had a fine time and appreciated the club's efforts. The event was intended to create a diversion from the Army post and it worked.

What we came to Lemoore for was a chance to fly the Vultee "Valiant" airplane, the BT-13. That opportunity came the following day. My instructor, Lt. Dorris, introduced himself. He was a likable fellow, fresh out of Advanced Flying School, this being his first class. He showed us how to get the Vultee started. This low wing monoplane had a self-starter and variable pitch propeller, much different from the Stearmans we were flying. I was assigned to C Flight.

Sundays were free time for "bunk fatigue," working on my photo album, studying, and letters. Writing home was tempting to put aside because of what seemed like a million other things to do first. But I didn't want to lose contact with Wes Parlee and Brad

Stewart and the folks back home. Sometimes on Sundays we had bull sessions, either sitting in our rooms or at the PX, or day rooms, where we drank Cokes and listened to tall stories. A sergeant told why he would rather be in a regular Air Corps outfit instead of doing these training classes. The boy across the hall told how he "spun in" (crashed) one day and was still convalescing.

Finally, we had our chance to fly the Vultee BT-13. The plane compared with a Stearman like a Packard compared with a Model T Ford. The pilot sat up high and could easily look in any direction. It seemed like a heavy battleship with wings. Thermals did not bother it as much as they did the Stearman. It flew smoothly and gracefully on maneuvers. My instructor told us, "Ten percent of this course will be flying and 90% using your head. You are supposed to know how to fly already. This phase is to adjust you to differing conditions."

One of the conditions we faced had nothing to do with flying. We had no air conditioning in our classrooms, with temperatures over 100 degrees. Wendell Hanson put it this way, "Some of the fellows are growing pointed tails and horns. They feel that hell could be no hotter, so they feel right at home. There is even a rumor that farmers have been missing their pitchforks." Later we measured 110 degrees in the shade, but the needle was pinned against the stop, so it must have been even hotter. It felt like someone was spraying my back with a blow torch.

At first, my flying seemed like the period at Primary when everything was thrown at me and I didn't know from day to day whether I would wash out. Five of us in C Flight shared one instructor. One student, I figured, would wash out because of his general attitude. Another almost washed out because he pulled the mixture control knob back by mistake while recovering from a simulated forced landing. That stopped the engine and the forced landing was nearly real.

On the ninth day I soloed after two and a half hours of flight with my instructor. It went this way. Lt. Dorris called our five together and said, "Today we'll stay in the pattern. I want to show you some landings." After four landings with me he got out and asked, "Do you think you can handle it alone?"

I replied, "Well, I can sure try!" So I flew it around the pattern twice, solo.

Next we started ground school with a maintenance class on the flight line, learning how to preflight an airplane and make periodic checks and even repairs. The instructor told us, "In combat, mechanics are not always available, so pilots are often called upon to make their own repairs."

We were required to have 16 hours of Link Trainer time before leaving Basic Flying School, intended to teach flying blind (on instruments), and also to smoothen our coordination, all with the use of a simple ground device.

The method of punishment for flying errors on the flight line was the "star system." We were given stars as demerits, costing us 25 cents apiece, the money to be used for our final party. My instructor gave me two stars for flying an incorrect pattern around the field, another for changing the prop pitch at the wrong time and then, while I was flying solo, I was awarded a few more. While taxiing for take-off I was so busy talking on my radio that I didn't see a plane coming in for a landing. It came rather close, so the radio boomed out, "Ship 206, take four stars for that."

Next Saturday at 4 pm we had open post. Cadets Johnny Harris, Jack Lepird, and I climbed into my car and sped off for Fresno. We obtained a hotel room and bought a good steak dinner. Still too early to do anything exciting, the three of us went to a movie, "Flight Lieutenant," a typical, faked, unauthentic picture. Next we stopped at the Rainbow for a dance or two. Somehow I never went much for going stag to a dance. That was about all for Saturday night. In the morning it was a pleasure to sleep in, lying on a thick mattress, then to take a nice hot shower, and have a waffle for breakfast. We drove down to Hanford for a swim in the pool. How nice, where water was not too plentiful, to stand in cold water up to one's neck.

The next day I flew every period from 7 am to noon. Boy, was I tired by night time! The Vultees were such a pleasure to fly that I became restless between flights. Lt. Dorris assigned me my first instrument ride. At 3,000 feet I put the hood over my head. The instruments had a lag, so it was not as easy as it looked. After ten minutes Lt. Dorris got bored and began practicing his acrobatics, which I enjoyed as much as he did.

The athletic director scheduled things so that after ground school on every other afternoon we would go into town for a swim. This served two purposes: first, we had a chance to cool off in the water, and second, we got out of athletics which would have meant hot exercises and running. Also, we got a pass from marching in the drill period. Believe me, swimming was something I really enjoyed!

Lt. Dorris spent most of one morning trying to arrange a dog fight with another instructor. We cadets could be washed out, without even a check ride, for doing that while flying solo, but the lieutenants could get away with it. Lt. Dorris showed me snap rolls, a snap and a half into a loop, and a half snap on top. It took him three times to get it right, though. I tried lazy eights solo. It was the closest to acrobatics I was allowed to do alone, and I wasn't sure even that was permissible, but it sure helped me develop coordination while producing diversion from the routine.

One day we had a track meet. The upper class competed with the lower class, warning us that, if we won, we might expect the worst for all of the next week. They were just waiting to leave for advanced training and would not have anything to do except make life miserable for us underclassmen. Fortunately for us, the upperclassmen won the track meet.

The Vultee Valiant BT-13

The cockpit seemed full of instruments.

CHAPTER 12
An Upperclassman

SOME DAYS WERE DIFFICULT. On one such off-day I just couldn't "keep my head out" (of my backside), a favorite expression of the cadets. I was scheduled to take my 20 hour check with the assistant flight commander, who had the reputation of being tough. When he talked to me afterward, I thought he was going to wash me out, send me to prison, and make me buy a new airplane. But surprise, surprise! He passed me.

At night we started night flying. Again, I had trouble. That time I couldn't see my instruments or controls in the darkness and my radio was out of order. But Lt. Dorris soloed me and it turned out to be fun after all. He said to our flight, "Flying will become different. We will be flying only at night for one week, then only cross country for a week, and just formation flying the next."

With that schedule Lemoore became less like an Army base and more like a country club. We could sleep until 9 am, attend two classes, and then fly for a couple of hours at night. In our spare time we could get in a few hours in the Link Trainer.

Night flying was the most exciting part of our training, requiring constant vigilance. Every few minutes, it seemed, someone encountered a close call. On the first night my radio acted up on me just when I needed it most. After an hour and a half the radio, lights, and everything electrical blew out, so I brought back the airplane. On the ground, Lt. Dorris sensed my problem and gave me the green light to land.

Our first cross country trip went from Lemoore to Clovis, to Porterville, to Wasco, to Avenal, and then back to Lemoore— about 250 miles long and lasting for two hours. Between Clovis and Porterville I flew fairly close to Rankin and saw a chance to do something exciting. So I veered off to Exeter field and then Rankin field, made a couple of vertical turns over Rankin, and continued on. I couldn't withstand the temptation to show off over the field where I spent so much sweat and worry in Primary Flying School.

On completion of our Aircraft Maintenance course the final exam went like this:

"What is prop wash?"

"It's what you hang on that wire between the aerial post and the fin."

"Very good! Now, how do you unfasten the right wing?"

"Drop the airplane in from about 50 feet."

"Correct."

Actually the course was serious and we learned a lot from it.

Our next cross country trip took me to Tracy. Our assignment was to find the correct field out of several nearby and make a landing there. Some cadets got a little too anxious and landed at wrong fields south of Tracy. The flight commander was really upset when he heard his students couldn't even land at the right field. Five cadets admitted landing at other fields and another wouldn't admit it. The whole flight had to spend several hours marching.

On my last daytime cross-country trip my instructor, Lt. Dorris, rode along in the back seat. Halfway through the trip I looked back and gasped, his head was back and his mouth open—sound asleep.

After landing I went up again, this time with the assistant flight commander for my 40 hour check. Good news! I passed it.

The next morning in daylight, Lt. Dorris showed me formation flying, which really required being on the ball.

After dark we flew a night cross country, much different than in daylight. The airway was as busy as San Fernando Road at change-of-shifts at Lockheed; 150 airplanes were flying from various schools in that area. Making things worse, San Joaquin Valley was having a partial blackout, affecting our ground observations. Our flight commander was really surprised that no one was killed on that night cross-country. But C Flight was lucky. Other than the time Cadet Hamm ran his pitot tube (part of the air speed indicator system) through an ambulance, we had no accidents.

Colonel Reddock, for some strange reason, gave us open post at 1:30 instead of the usual 4:00 pm. Jim Hamer, another cadet, and I set out in my car for Los Angeles. Somewhere between Corcoran and Earlimart the inserts in my engine overheated and froze. I limped into Delano, left the car with a mechanic, and we hitchhiked down to Los Angeles.

Wes Parlee was home from Santa Ana, so he and I along with Julian Tucker drove around town like old times. We visited Melvin Heflinger, who was still instructing at Rankin, and then the Walters girls. I was amazed to see the Lockheed Aircraft plant ringed with smoke pots to provide a smoke screen in the event of an air raid. Lockheed P-38s were thick around there.

My brother was working for Lockheed, waiting for his Navy appointment. He told me of his wedding plans, to be married about November 1st, and he asked me to be his best man. I replied that I would be honored if I could get away. As it turned out, I was stationed at Greenville, South Carolina in November, unable to attend the wedding.

I met Jim Hamer at Los Feliz and Riverside Drive and we rode back to Lemoore in his car.

Our next phase of training was formation flying. Doing it solo required my attention every second. Lt. Dorris spent some time with his students in the air and, after a while, gave a signal and we peeled off, one after another at five second intervals. It evolved into a rat race and a lot of fun. An enlisted man riding with Lt. Dorris didn't go much for the peel-offs, but he enjoyed the rest of it.

The next day we practiced formation flying again. When Lt. Dorris signaled for the peel-off, down he went, and I followed. This eventually turned into a dog fight. I tried to keep on my instructor's tail. We both had about 40 degrees of flaps down and full throttle on. When I began overtaking him in a tight circle, I throttled back to avoid a collision. Trying to get back in the circle, I pulled back on the stick, stalled out, and went into a spin, but recovered. After a few more acrobatics we went back into formation.

On August 12th General Couzins arrived at Lemoore to present our new wing flag. We had a big parade to make the formalities complete. I was fortunate to be a part of the color guard. How interesting it was to be up close and see how those old generals and colonels became fidgety and flustered. Six flying officers passed out while standing at attention but none of the cadets did. They couldn't afford to, under penalty of being washed out.

Sometimes things didn't work out as planned. During a dual instrument ride, while I had a black hood covering me, the hood ripped off. It happened while I was practicing recovery from a tail spin and I couldn't see the instruments. Somehow I recovered from the spin, but we couldn't do any more "hood" flying, so Lt. Dorris told me to do a snap roll. I tried one; it was OK except my speed was too high at 140 mph. At that speed, the vertical stabilizer could come off in a snap roll, I was told. Well, a miss is as good as a mile, they say! Then he told me to do a snap and a half, followed by a split S and ending with a loop, at a slower speed of course. I tried and it worked OK. Then, I did a slow roll.

That was my first experience doing acrobatics in the Vultee BT-13 which, we were told was not built for acrobatics but originally was intended as a dive bomber. By the time it reached production, however, better planes were available, one being the Douglas Dauntless dive bomber. So the Vultee was sent to the training command. The Air Force named its Dauntless the A-24. Little did I know at that time, before the war was over I would be flying the A-24, but not for the purpose of dive bombing. It was a wonderful airplane to fly.

My next challenge was in formation flying at night. All the pilot could see were three lights, one on each wing tip plus the fin. Our object was to draw imaginary lines between those three lights, and then figure out the attitude of the lead ship, and finally duplicate that attitude. Two and a half hours of that was really hard work.

In the afternoon I had "beam instrument" flying, which meant flying beneath the hood and listening to the Morse code N's and A's of the Fresno radio range, which told the pilot whether he was on the right side or the left of the radio beam running down the civil airway, not as easy as it might seem. On the way home Lt. Dorris hedge-hopped over fences and trees.

On Saturday I declined my usual open post in Fresno. It didn't seem reasonable to blow so much money on weekends. Instead, I rode as far as Delano with Jim Hamer, who was making his usual trek to Los Angeles. At Delano I picked up my car at the garage where I had left it earlier and brought it back to the post. It cost me $20.95 to replace the inserts in the engine. Going to bed on my Army cot that Saturday night was eerie, sleeping all alone in an empty barrack.

We finished our flying at Lemoore by practice in turbulent air conditions, and then by flying cross country on instruments the next day. Amazingly, by flying a certain compass course for a planned number of minutes, a pilot could hit a town right on the nose. That completed my 80 hour requirement at Basic Flying School.

High point of the day was the flight party that evening, paid for by the star system and held at the California Hotel in Fresno. The cadets and officers all behaved like gentlemen. In the past, we were told, such parties had been like some American Legion Conventions, with a couple hundred dollars' worth of furniture broken up. But we kept our heads this time.

With a 48-hour pass, most of the cadets lit out for Los Angeles, San Francisco, and all sorts of places. I drove up to Yosemite National Park which I had not seen; Dick Heddens and Johnny Harris went with me. What a sight it was. When we rounded the turn in the road and saw those slick, vertical rock walls of the valley far below, with Half Dome in the distance, it was indeed a thrill. The national parks were nice to men in the service, offering free admission. Lodging was only half price, but the meals were high priced. Returning to the post, bull sessions started up. Everyone had a story to tell. Anything could happen off base and often it did.

On the following Monday, we should have been given open post, as there was nothing more for us to do at Lemoore. Unfortunately, about 50 cadets were late in getting back from open post over the weekend. Also, we had left the barracks in a mess during the weekend. Added to that, our mess officer was angry with us for something we did or did not do, so we got stuck on the post. Most of the cadets were flat broke anyway, so open post would have been of no benefit.

When we did get out, Johnny Harris and I went to a movie while Jim Hamer visited his new girlfriend.

We were late in leaving Lemoore because someone burned down the dodo's barrack. Unfortunately, C Flight's orderly room was in that barrack and the fire started in the orderly room, so the commandant held C Flight responsible and questioned us one by one. We finally got away by 3:00 pm. On the way south, one of my tires blew out on Highway 99, so I continued on home with the spare.

How nice to sleep at home in Pasadena! I spent the first half of the next morning looking for a second hand tire but couldn't find one, so I spent the second half selling the car. The best I could get was $100. After my insurance refund, I ended up with $111.70 cash.

I joined up with my roommate, Jim Hamer; we boarded a Greyhound bus and headed for Phoenix. It was a hectic trip. The bus couldn't go over 40 mph and the driver got a ticket. People were standing in the aisles. After a bouncy night with practically no sleep, we arrived late at Williams Field, Chandler, Arizona.

Dave Hayward felt right at home in the Vultee BT-13.

The Link Trainer was often frustrating.

CHAPTER 13
Assignment at Dinjan

IT IS DIFFICULT TO say what part of our training at Tulare and Lemoore was most valuable to me when I served overseas with the 22nd Bomb Squadron. Certainly the pilot training was essential. Discipline, patience, and hard work played a role too. The intensity of our training left little or no free time. In that respect, however, combat conditions were quite different. Flying missions for an average of once a week left a lot of time on my hands and there wasn't much to do when not flying, so I broke the fundamental rule: "Don't ever volunteer for anything."

Shortly after my arrival in India a request came from headquarters for our squadron to send a single plane and crew to Assam Province for a series of single-plane raids on Japanese-held installations in northern Burma. At that time I was serving my apprenticeship as copilot for Lt. Patrick Ham. He volunteered to go on the special assignment and asked if I wanted to go along as his copilot. I thought, *It sounds like an adventure. Why not?* And I agreed to go with him.

The 22nd Bomb Squadron flew 169 missions from India between December 1942 and January 1944. Seventeen of them were flown by a single B-25 medium bomber. I flew on four of those missions, from Dinjan in the northeastern part of India. Single-plane missions were best suited for reconnaissance or just getting in and out of hot spots as undetected as possible.

On April 28, 1943, Pat Ham flew our plane to Dinjan, an Allied airfield along the Brahmaputra River, where the Himalayas of Tibet rise in the west and the Patkai Range of

Burma lies to the east. Stepping out of the airplane I thought, *Wow! I'm standing at our furthest outpost in India.*

Looking around, I saw tea plantations. A squadron of P-40s from the 51st Fighter Group waited on the airfield, with their pilots seated in the cockpits ready to be called to scramble if enemy aircraft should approach. Assam was the "jumping off" spot for Allied supplies flown over the Hump to China, most of which departed from Chabua nearby.

Adding to the drama, a Jeep picked up Pat, our navigator-bombardier Carl Wildner, and me and drove us to a tea planter's bungalow, built on stilts, with screening all around the structure's four sides. A well-trained Indian bearer met us as we entered and soon served us tea, waiting on our every need. I felt I could be living in a novel by Somerset Maugham, a popular writer of British life in Southeast Asia.

In the cool of the evening we three strolled along a dirt road through the tea plantation. A row of tall bamboo trees served as a wind screen on one side of the road as we told stories. Our pilot, Pat Ham, was a member of Project 157, the group who flew 26 B-25s from Florida to India in May 1942, before Ascension Island was available as a refueling stop. Carl Wildner was a navigator on the famous Doolittle raid on Japan in April 1942. What an experience I was having!

One day while at Dinjan, I visited with a P-40 pilot who was on alert. He had to sit in the cockpit of his plane, in the hot India sun, with his crew chief standing by to help him get his engine started when the time came. Sandwiches were brought to him at mid-day. In the event of an alert, his orders were to take off immediately, climb to a designated altitude in "Cast 13," a section on his grid map, and wait for further orders. He hadn't seen enemy action yet but was eager to do so.

Boredom, it seemed, was part of a fighter pilot's life—just waiting, with more than enough excitement at other times to make up for it. What stroke of fate sent me to fly bombers, and for that young man to fly fighters? Possibly my six feet one inch height had something to do with it. Or could it be temperament? Or just that we were expected to go where we were needed at the time? Our training until late in the program was much the same for both bomber and fighter pilots. Soon, I might see that P-40 pilot again, but under different circumstances.

Our first single-plane raid out of Dinjan was on April 30th to Mohnyin, Burma, 75 miles south of the Japanese stronghold at Myitkyina (pronounced Mitch'-en-aw). Our mission was to attack enemy installations along the railroad, with the luxury of escort by P-40 aircraft stationed at Dinjan. Crossing the mountains in a southeasterly direction, I took pictures of the P-40s. Although they had no need to take action against an enemy that day, those P-40s were a real comfort to have along. Japanese fighters did not choose to attack us.

Prior to each mission we were informed how many fighter planes we might find in the area, but often found either the enemy fighters had moved out or just chose to avoid us. Those intelligence reports were often out of date, but we had to assume the worst, that they were correct. The enemy was doing a lot of staging—moving from place to place to make maximum coverage with their planes. That day, our mission was short, just 2 ½ hours. We encountered no problems.

The following day we flew a 2 hour 20 minute mission to Hopin, Burma, also along the railroad line but only 60 miles from Myitkyina. Returning to Dinjan, a hearty lunch awaited us. That afternoon we took off for another mission, our third into northern Burma, a "search and destroy" mission for enemy targets of opportunity along the railroad. Once again, we encountered no problems.

On May 3rd we flew the last of our single-plane raids into northern Burma. That time it was a 2 hour and 10 minute mission to Namti, located along the railroad only 18 miles from the enemy stronghold at Myitkyina. *Certainly*, I thought, *we had alerted the Japanese by then and surely they would find us that day.* We knew the Japanese brought their fighter planes into that area because, at the time, they were attacking our transport planes flying over the Hump. Evidently, we lucked out and caught the enemy again when their planes were somewhere else, as we had the good fortune of avoiding them a fourth time.

Back at the tea planter's bungalow near the Dinjan airfield, at the end of the day, it sure felt good being served royally by our obedient Indian bearer.

Had those missions been flown out of our base at Chakulia, a formal debriefing would have transpired, probing for details of specific targets and explanations of results. However, as we were just one aircraft, we escaped that type of debriefing and I learned little about the results at that time. As to whether the missions were successful, all four missions went off as planned. We found our targets, made our bomb runs, left the targets in dust and smoke, and returned safely to Dinjan. If we were fired upon, I didn't see it.

On May 4th I returned to Chakulia, ready to resume my place in the regular rotation of mission assignments to central Burma. But what an experience my days at Dinjan were!

After the war, when more records became available, I learned much more about the situation in north Burma in early 1943 and how our four missions fit into the overall situation.

In February of that year two friendly ground operations were going on in northern Burma. British Major General Orde Wingate led a force of native Chindit warriors into Burma in a campaign to harass the Japanese through jungle warfare. His goals were to disrupt enemy supply lines, gather intelligence, rescue downed airmen, and identify targets for the U.S. Air Force to attack along the Japanese supply route to their main base at Myitkyina. General Wingate's forces remained in northern Burma through March 1943.

Also in February, the U.S. Office of Strategic Services (OSS) sent to northern Burma a group known as Detachment 101. Their aim was to disrupt Japanese air operations from Myitkyina, where the Japanese were attacking U.S. cargo planes flying supplies over the Hump to China. Detachment 101 planned to accomplish this by cutting rail lines and blowing up bridges south of the city, thereby cutting off supplies to Myitkyina. Their main force left Burma late in February, but some elements remained until June of 1943.

As the result of intelligence gained by the Wingate and OSS groups, on March 2nd the 490th Bomb Squadron, sister squadron to the 22nd Bomb Squadron, sent eight B-25 medium bombers to Myitkyina and attacked enemy barracks and installations in the center of town. This was followed on March 6th by twelve B-25s from the 491st Bomb Squadron, another sister squadron of the 22nd, staging a raid on Myitkyina, this time attacking buildings, barracks, and supply dumps there.

In the meantime, P-40 aircraft from the 51st Fighter Group at Dinjan maintained a series of attacks on enemy installations in the Myitkyina area.

The records now provide some details on the single-plane B-25 raids carried out by the 22nd Bomb Squadron from April 30th to May 3rd, in which I participated.

On May 1st, at Hopin, Burma, our lone B-25 was escorted by four P-40 fighter aircraft. We carried eight 300 pound bombs and thirty seven fragmentation bombs. Ninety percent of the bombs fell in the target area and started 12 fires, several with large columns of black smoke. 20 mm or 37 mm anti-aircraft fire was encountered at Mingon, which was then bombed and the firing from the ground ceased.

On May 3rd, at Namti, Burma, we had three P-40 escort planes and we carried eight 300 pound demolition bombs. Three direct hits and five near misses destroyed six railroad cars. After the attack we made a reconnaissance over Myitkyina and observed two sunken river steamers and a destroyed enemy staff car. The roads and bridges appeared to be in well-traveled condition, good targets for a future raid.

Our bearer waited on our every need.

Dave Hayward took these photos of the P-40 escort from the window of his B-25.

CHAPTER 14
Advanced Flying School

MY FIRST IMPRESSION OF Arizona's Williams Field was not very good, having arrived there on a blazing day in late August 1942. Sure, we could walk around without ties and just leave our collars open and there was no silly class system or hazing. We were treated like the gentlemen we were supposed to be. How odd, the hazing business, that the government would spend months of time and effort on us and then practically admit failure by treating us like imbeciles.

As I was walking to the PX, a car pulled up and who should it be but "Lindy," Lt. James Oscar Lindberg, a friend and neighbor who lived near us on Orange Grove Avenue in Pasadena. He was my brother's best friend, so I saw a lot of Lindy back home. I knew he was at Williams Field and hoped he would be my instructor. That didn't happen, but we stayed in contact anyway.

Never since joining the Army had I slept or eaten so much. The food was served on huge trays, out of large pots with big ladles. It seemed impossible to avoid taking too much. Rather than seeing good food go to waste, the cadets stuffed themselves, leaving the mess hall with bulging stomachs. It was really good food, too, with lots of steaks and fruit and milk, and at a time when the public was severely restricted in that way.

Five cadets were assigned to my instructor, as before. One of the five was Tom Harmon, the All American football player from the University of Michigan. In spite of his fame on the football field, he seemed to be just a regular guy and didn't try to be anything else.

I was in Lindy's squadron and barely missed landing him as my instructor. But mine, Lt. Grumman, was a nice person whom I liked. He gave me a ride in an AT-17, a twin engine airplane built by Cessna. It seemed like just a big Piper Cub, flying at 90 to 100 mph, fabric covered, rather cheap and flimsy to look at, and easy to fly. We called it the "Bamboo Bomber."

My flying at first was not very good; a flashback to my experience in both Primary and Basic Flying Schools when it seemed like everything was thrown at me at once. But I figured things would get better.

Williams Field was agreeable, except for the insect problem. Sitting on the edge of my bed one day I counted five flies within one square foot on the blanket. The mosquitoes were even worse; they left welts.

To my surprise, Lt. Grumman sent Cadet Haskell and me up for a solo flight. For the first two hours, Haskell was assigned as pilot with me as copilot. After two hours, we would trade places. Haskell made his takeoff alright and two landings but, unfortunately, on his second landing he rolled past the mat, onto the desert and ripped open the right wing on a greasewood tree. It happened at an auxiliary field. Our instructor took Haskell back to the base and, after five hours, another lieutenant came for me. Fortunately, Haskell did not wash out for his misjudgment. In fact, a few weeks later he stood next to me as we graduated.

Lt. Grumman got around to soloing me. We flew down to Casa Grande field where another cadet and I acted as each other's copilot while the other one soloed. My solo flight went along just fine. No sooner did I get back than I had to act as copilot for another cadet.

We received no credit for flight time while sitting as copilot in training, yet it had one redeeming value—it taught me how the pilot's performance appears to other people in the plane. Under combat conditions I found some pilots to be very nervous while flying, particularly those who smoked or drank excessively. Crews felt uneasy with nervous pilots. As a result, I tried my best to present a calm appearance while flying as pilot and was rewarded by the confidence of my crew members.

Our athletic program included an obstacle course, hurdling tree trunks, vaulting over fences, and scaling walls. At the end of the course, the cool waters of the swimming pool were mighty, mighty inviting.

As days went by, my flight time in the AT-17 increased to ten hours. I was practicing takeoffs and landings at Casa Grande auxiliary field when I noticed my right engine cutting out on takeoff. The control ship on the ground radioed up to me to land as soon as possible, which I did. Who should walk up to me but my old neighbor and friend, Lindy? He said my engine sounded like it would never get the plane off the ground. The mechanic checked it out and found nothing wrong, so I took off again, but it continued to cut out on takeoff. It became no worse so I flew the ship back to our base at Williams Field.

My instructor in Theory of Bombing class announced, "Someone stole a Norden bomb site this morning." It was no small matter. A search was made. He continued, "The person who checked it out gave a false name." The next day we learned that the bomb site turned out to be "stolen" by the FBI as an efficiency test. The OD (Officer of the Day) had the bomb site in his car the whole time. It taught us all a lesson. After that, a cadet had to be known by about six men before he could check out a bomb site.

Jim Hamer, my roommate, had a crash landing that day. He blew a tire on takeoff but lifted the plane off the ground, circled the field, and made a one-wheel landing. The plane was badly damaged in landing but Jim was not injured.

One day I chatted with some Chinese cadets. They already had 100 hours of flight time, had gone through a military academy, and were now training here in America. In their entire detachment only three spoke English fluently. One was born in San Francisco, one in Hawaii, and the other in the Philippines. All the rest knew just a few words they picked up in four weeks of ground school.

One of the cadets said to me, "We came from Hunan Province, not far from the AVG (American Volunteer Group—the Flying Tigers) headquarters, near Jimmy Doolittle's base for bombing Japan."

At our dinner table, I noticed one Chinese filling his glass of milk with a heaping tablespoon of sugar and drinking it. I asked him about it and he replied, "Hong Kong." I asked him how he liked our food. He held up a piece of chocolate cake and replied, "This best." The Flight Surgeon next to me observed our conversation and added, "These Chinese are all sugar-starved, and here in America they frequently buy up boxes of candy at a time to eat." I found the Chinese to be really nice. Not surprising, their tact and manners went back for centuries. Ho Han Ching gave me his photograph, taken at the Kunming airfield in Yunnan Province, China.

The cadets at Williams Field had problems and learned to deal with them. Three cadets had wheels fall off their airplanes and a few more made crash landings because their landing gear would not come down. In our own flight, at least four cadets were close to washing out due to cockpit procedure or landings. Instrument flying was more difficult in the AT-17. It was hard to hold constant altitude in turns. The plane spiraled (dove) in right turns and zoomed (climbed) in left turns. The Vultee was easier because it had dihedral (sloping) in the wings to make it self-stabilizing in rough air. The air was so bumpy that formation flying was difficult as well. That was not a fault of the airplane—just another problem we cadets had to cope with.

*Cessna AT-17, which the cadets called
the "Bamboo Bomber."*

*Cadet Ho Han Ching
gave Dave Hayward
this autographed
photo, taken at
Kunming, China.*

CHAPTER 15
Cross-Country Flying

CLASS 42-J STARTED DOING cross-country flying. One cadet took off only to run into clouds and fog, finally getting lost. He tried to find his destination by the radio beam, but just got more mixed up. Finally he set down at Douglas near the Mexican border, refueled, and came back to the base.

Our flight made a cross-country trip to Salome and Gila Bend; I was copilot that time. One of the other planes had trouble; Cadet Fite was the pilot and Tom Harmon was copilot. Their ship checked in at Salome but on the next leg, to Gila Bend, Fite must have gotten lost or forced down, because the ship never returned to Williams Field. Instructors searched all night but had no luck finding them.

The story came out next day. Fite and Harmon landed that night on the shores of the Gulf of California in Mexico. Fite reported, "My compass was out of order and my right engine conked out, requiring me to make a forced landing. I stayed with the ship while Harmon hitchhiked into town. I told him to notify the American consul and call up Williams Field with the report."

Two instructors flew down in AT-6s to pick up Fite and Harmon, and then the colonel flew down to inspect the ship. Fite had landed "wheels up" and damaged the propellers. We learned the next day that Fite washed out for getting lost, along with two upperclassmen who "buzzed" (low level flying) when they had just three hours of flying to go before getting their wings (graduation).

Shortly after midnight, our group reported to the flight line to begin night flying. I flew a BT-13 Vultee to an auxiliary field and met my instructor there. Night flying in an AT-17 was like flying around in a bus. With reduced turbulence after dark, flying seemed easier, the landings smoother, and the whole flight more comfortable. I got to bed about 6:00 am.

The next night, it seemed, we spent the darkness just flying around in circles. Cadets Gmitro and Goldberg kept the radio quite busy reporting their engines heating up. Time and again they called the control ship to find out what to do. Finally, after everyone got tired of hearing "Coolidge Control from 154, Blah! Blah! Blah!" someone cut in and said, "Take it easy, 154." To that Goldberg muttered back, "Everything's all messed up." We welcomed the variation from formality of radio communication but they were going a little too far.

On the following night we had another informal radio conversation. I flew as pilot to Phoenix, out the "light line" for a while and then back. Then I flew as copilot for a trip to Tucson and back. Down by Tucson, Cadet Ed Foster is supposed to have made a great radio address. "Earth to Mars, go ahead. Mars to Earth go ahead. Attention all South American countries! Tom Harmon is on a cross-country trip. Be on the watch for him. That is all."

I thought that was a cruel trick to play on a nice guy who was trying his best to fit in with the rest of us, but it made for a few laughs, at Harmon's expense of course. Foster denied having made the speech. Who will ever know?

What I did know, however, was that three days later, while on a cross-country trip to Ashfork and back, Ed Foster went on a singing spree over the radio. This time—no question about it. The singing was awful. Wendell Hanson walked up to him after the flight and commented, "Ed, I went along with your singing off key but when you flubbed the words to the Air Force Song, it was too much." As I mentioned previously, Wendell and I were at the same posts since Santa Ana and became good friends.

We practiced formation flying in the following morning before dawn. Lt. Grumman gave us instructions to watch for flashlight signals from the lead ship. A steady light signified "Fly further away" and a flashing light meant "Come closer." Apparently Lt. Grumman got the signals mixed because 99% of the time we had room for ten airplanes to fly between our ships, ten times too much. Finally, he got disgusted and went to sleep while his student flew him around, leading the formation. I wondered, *Why didn't Lt. Grumman try the radio to get his message across?*

Mysteriously, one day we were summoned to the flight line and sent right up in the air. All went well until entering the traffic pattern for landing. Everything got mixed up. Pilots cut other pilots out of the pattern, jamming up in groups and violating rule after rule. Each time we called for landing instructions the tower told us "Go around." I went around eleven times and was really anxious to escape the rat race. When I did get down, I learned our instructors and the tower deliberately messed up the landing pattern to show the colonel they needed better landing facilities.

One advantage of cross-country trips was the opportunity to see beautiful countryside. One afternoon I took in Ashfork and Winslow—that trip was easily the most scenic so far. I flew over a miniature Grand Canyon, cut magnificently into a flat-topped mesa. We later flew over a high plateau, thick with evergreen trees. Near Winslow, I gazed with awe at the Meteor Crater.

I was so busy I forgot to apply for a pass that weekend, so I slept until noon and indulged in a chicken dinner with all the trimmings. In town, the cadets had to pay about $2.50 for a good dinner, and even then the steaks were not always tender. Our food on the base was as good as could be had.

On October 4th I wrote a letter to my family back home—to dad and Stewart at the Orange Grove Avenue home in Pasadena. I wrote, "I'm sure glad you are going to work at civil defense, dad. I'm also glad to hear of your raise at Lockheed, Stewart. They should have you as one of their vice presidents before long."

I told them both about my cross-country trips over the beautiful Arizona desert. I told them about flying through the darkness of night and spotting our destination below. I described instrument flying, "I could have sworn up and down that I was flying the ship banked about 45 degrees, because the seat seemed to be skidding out from under me, but the instruments said we were flying straight and level. The pilot who does not believe his instruments is very foolish."

I went on to say, "Right now Wendell Hanson and I are waiting for a couple of Chinese cadets to come up to our room so we can take them to the show. Next Saturday they are going to take us to a Chinese restaurant in town for some real Chinese food." As it turned out, dinner with the Chinese was postponed, but on the Friday before, two Chinese friends came to my room for a visit. They had just flunked their English exam, so my roommate and I tried to help them out as best we could.

In the ready room the next day our flight commander announced, "Men, you've now had almost 200 hours of flying time, but today you'll begin flying the first 'real' airplane, the North American AT-6. It's really a wonderful airplane if you treat it right." He was correct. After my first ride with Lt. Grumman I was surprised with its ease of handling and remarkable results. We shot several landings and some chandelles and steep turns. A sweet airplane it was.

After two days flying the Phoenix "beam," I found it easier each time and realized what an important aid it was to navigation. Strangely, the beam bent to avoid mountains. The southeast leg of the beam was supposed to travel over Superstition Mountain, but it bent to the south and went right down the valley, nearly passing over Williams Field.

I flew over Superstition Mountain many times, scanning the terrain for clues of the Lost Dutchman Mine, supposedly hidden down there somewhere. Stories of the lost treasure of Superstition Mountain added a spice to what we were doing.

The next day I soloed in the AT-6. All three landings were bouncy, though, because I didn't get the stick back just right. That was the same trouble I had with the Stearman in Primary Flying School, not much different when it came to landing. The AT-6's fault was that its narrow landing gear made it more susceptible to ground looping. We had to be gentle in landing the plane. Two years later I embarrassed myself by doing a ground loop in an AT-6.

Sundays were days of relaxation. Cadets returning from open post adventures had wild tales to tell. Some were unbelievable. They played pranks on one another, too. Dick Heddens fixed Ed Foster's bed so it would break down when he came back from town. That resulted in a big "hullabaloo," all in fun.

At times our training got monotonous, doing the same exercises and practicing the same maneuvers hour after hour. One day I added a little history to my flight. I flew down to the Casa Grande ruin, near the town of Coolidge, and made a close inspection of it from the air. I remember being so impressed with the famous pre-Columbian building.

We practiced aerial gunnery at the Ajo Gunnery Range. It seemed to be more like legalized "buzzing." We were supposed to "peel off" at 800 feet and dive down to about 50 feet off the ground at 160 to 180 mph. We were lucky if we hit the target at all. No one bothered to put bull's-eyes on the targets. Some fellows shot 1,000 rounds without even hitting the target.

Fortunately, our scores were not a determining factor in whether we would wash out of the program.

Next, we shot skeet for the first time, my first experience with firing a shotgun. The program was intended to teach us how to fire at a moving target. *It should be easy*, I thought, *just one piece of shot should break a clay pigeon.* I broke 11 of the 25 clay pigeons that were fired, not too bad for a first try. But, man! Those shotguns could sure kick against your shoulder. After that, I learned to wear my leather jacket when shooting skeet.

The promised dinner with the Chinese cadets finally happened. They took Wendell Hanson and me out to a restaurant on the south side of Phoenix, where we ate real Chinese food, complete with chop sticks. Quite a few Chinese cadets were there. Actually, I didn't care much for the food, not being used to it, but we tried to show appreciation. After dinner we took our Chinese hosts to Encanto Park and rode around in motor boats, and then we had a canoe race. Returning to the base, Wendell and I joined the other cadets who were watching a performance put on by the entertainer Jack Benny.

Our flight continued with aerial gunnery practice, this time with the target going one way and my plane going the other. My guns jammed the first time, I missed the second, and I failed to hear about the rest. That kind of aerial gunnery sure beat shooting at ground targets, as it taught the pilot more about leading the target. In either case, luck seemed to determine one's score.

Approaching the end of our training at Williams Field, cadets learned that those who had gunnery practice would go next to Greenville, South Carolina, for training in the B-25 Mitchell medium bomber. Cadets without gunnery practice would go to Florida for B-17 heavy bomber training.

Our big day came on Friday, October 30, 1942, graduation day. I almost missed it because I couldn't get my dress uniform out of the cleaners, but finally did and made it to the ceremony on time. We lined up in alphabetical order. Near where I stood were Jim Hamer, Wendell Hanson, Tom Harmon, John Haskell, David Hayward, and Dick Heddens.

Ed Foster was there, in spite of his clowning around on the radio. Gmitro and Goldberg, who had so much trouble that night on cross-country, were also present. So were others whom I would know later at Greenville and in the 22nd Bomb Squadron in India and China: Wayne Craven, Colin Campbell, Dick DuBois, Mike Russell, and Elmer Thompson. We received our pilot's wings and commissions as second lieutenants in the Army Air Corps.

The graduation ceremony was simple but impressive. No flags were flying and no formations of planes flew overhead. It was a short, to-the-point ceremony. During the rest of the day cadets received their military orders, cleared out their things and packed up to leave.

Jim Hamer and I used POV (privately owned conveyance) to go to our next assignment, which gave us eight days of travel time.

The North American Aviation AT-6 advanced trainer

Cadet Ed Foster is "clowning around" with an empty practice bomb.

The day all cadets were waiting for

Williams Field Army Advanced

Flying School

Chandler, Arizona

Announces the Graduation of

Class 42-J

Pilots

Friday morning, October thirtieth

Nineteen Hundred and Forty-two

Williams Field

Look, folks, I made it!

CHAPTER 16
Between Assignments

JIM HAMER AND I traveled home for the 8 day break, not in a "personal" conveyance but aboard a commercial airliner. Evidently the "personal" in POV meant "personally acquired." Arriving home I found a job to do. Stewart was living in Alhambra and on that day was moving dad from his house on Orange Grove Avenue to a small unit in a court on El Molino Avenue in Pasadena. The manager of the court was an elderly man who would look in on dad and take care of any needs he couldn't handle himself.

At noontime Stewart drove me to Burbank to meet his bride-to-be. Alice was a nice lady and I wished them the best. Stewart dropped me off at Jim Hamer's house in Eagle Rock, where I met his mother and we had dinner together. Then, Jim and I drove to Long Beach and inquired of the Ferry Command if we could get a ride to South Carolina, but it was no deal. We drove to Santa Ana where the cadets were having their Sunday parade. The place had expanded beyond all belief since we were there. I was most impressed with what the Army could do in just of a few months.

The next day I was busy, with a visit first to Fletcher Aircraft Schools in Burbank; few of the old gang were left. My second visit was to Orban Lumber Company, my first job out of school. I started work there while participating in a "student day at the office" program. They kept me on for a while but then let me go. Was I not doing the job or were they just cutting back on expense? To this day I don't know the reason. On the day of my visit, perhaps I was thinking, *Look at me now. I'm a second lieutenant, wearing an impressive uniform and a pair of pilot's wings. I'm a success!*

On my second day of visits, I conveniently dropped in on the Jacobs family about dinner time. Their son Don was away in the Army, but their daughter Mary Lou was home. She married the soldier from Texas three weeks previously, who was off in Europe in a battle zone.

Mary Lou and I were long-time friends. I picked her up in my car each school day for a ride to Pasadena Junior College, and brought her home again at the end of the day. The Jacobs were grateful for that and made me aware of their liquor cabinet in the kitchen. I spent a lot of time at the Jacobs' house, not because of the liquor cabinet, but because they were genuinely pleasant to be with. Another good friend of mine, Elwood Davis, lived across the street from them. That's how I became acquainted with the Jacobs. After dinner I took Mary Lou to a stage play in Los Angeles called "Hey, Rookie," put on by the Fort MacArthur Boys. The two of us got a kick out of it, as we were both Army-minded.

I called Brad Stewart's number and found he was coming home that night, so I met with him and his folks. Another friend, Bill Dootson, a flying ensign, and a draftee named Lynn Wallace showed up and the four of us made the rounds of Los Angeles. Bill and I brought favorable glances from passersby to see a lieutenant pilot of the Army Air Corps with an ensign pilot of the U.S. Navy, walking shoulder to shoulder. At that time the Army and Navy had the reputation of not getting along very well together. We may have started the new trend of togetherness between branches of the service.

I was still enjoying my 8-day break. In the morning Jim Hamer came over to my house on El Molino Avenue and we rode around for most of the day. Late afternoon, he took me to his house for dinner and Mrs. Hamer's wonderful hospitality and kindliness. Jim's sister, Eleanor, had come home from Berkeley. She and I went out in the evening and I enjoyed her company. We agreed to write to each other.

Jim and I left his house early the next morning, headed for our assignment in Greenville, South Carolina. In those days travel was not easy. At Burbank airport, fog held up our flight for an hour, but we finally boarded an American Airlines flight. At El Paso, our onward connection was cancelled due to a hurricane in the Gulf of Mexico. We hopped on a train for Fort Worth and snagged two of its last seats, lucking into comfortable Pullmans. It was a good night's sleep, although we stopped at every little cattle town. At Fort Worth we secured an onward flight, arriving in Greenville just before dawn November 8th, seven hours late.

Brad Stewart was home on leave from the Coast Guard.

CHAPTER 17
The B-25 Mitchell Bomber

GREENVILLE'S AIR BASE WAS situated on rolling country in South Carolina and spread out over many acres. What a difference—pilots, navigators, bombardiers or gunner's proudly wearing their wings. We encountered a problem getting from the BOQ (bachelor officer's quarters) to the squadron buildings, officers mess, and other places. But I soon found the enlisted men were obliging and worked diligently to aid us officers. They provided Jeep service whenever needed. The sergeants in headquarters used the word "Sir" in almost every sentence. In addition, this was the first post not situated on reclaimed desert.

The next day I got my assignments: flying the B-25s with twelve students per instructor. Unfortunately, some men recently sent out to combat returned for more time, thus crimping our flying in the first week. Our squadron, the 472nd, had only seven B-25s, so it was apparent we would have difficulty getting flying time.

My instructor, Lt. Kempster, called his twelve students together and cautioned us. "The most eager men will be pilots while the others will be copilots." *That should keep us on the ball*, I thought.

Our late arrival that Sunday had consequences. I would have to write a letter to the general of the Third Air Force and possibly receive a fine. Also, my travel pay would be held up—quite inconvenient.

I practiced in the Link Trainer that afternoon, the closest to flying so far. However, Lt. Kempster did show me cockpit procedure in a B-25. The pilot's position was the best I had seen, quite comfortable, with controls easily within reach, an efficiently designed airplane.

The Flight Surgeon called me back for a recheck on my physical exam. He said I had too much albumin in my urinalysis, so I worried about that. Could I have come this far and get rejected over a matter of urine? I could be grounded.

After dinner I asked a pilot if he had room for a passenger that night. He said, "Yes, come on along." So I had my first ride in a B-25. It felt like a four-room house, with hallways inside. I spent most of my time sitting comfortably in the green house (the windowed nose area of the plane), listening to broadcast radio stations.

Two important things happened next day. The Flight Surgeon checked me out satisfactorily and the Finance Officer gave me my delinquent travel pay. What a relief!

On the more exciting side, Jim Hamer almost started the Civil War over again. He and I were in the PX (Post Exchange). Jim expressed his belief that racial prejudice was the most foolish thing about the South. He turned to a civilian worker and said, "I come from California and back there we don't care whether Sherman marched through Georgia or not."

The man turned red and countered, "Mister, down here we don't think that's very funny." It just about started a fight.

It was pretty clear to me that we would be with the B-25s for a long time. Since a pilot was to be chosen for his ability over the copilot, I was determined to make an intensive study of the airplane. I arranged for an older pilot to spend two hours showing me emergency systems and explain the important controls. I then practiced with a blindfold test for an hour by myself. After dinner someone showed me how to operate a power-driven gun turret, and I spent another hour after ground school in the pilot's compartment. After Link Trainer time I began reading the operating procedures published by North American Aviation.

Our group also spent time in the Bomb Trainer, giving us an understanding of the bombardier's function. At the same time there was an exhibition of incendiary bombs, but I missed it by being at the Bomb Trainer. For the rest of the day Jim Hamer and I studied B-25 technical orders and spent more time in the plane's cockpit. I still had no flying time, but by the next Monday the combat crews were expected to be gone and the schedule should be returned to normal.

After dinner on the following day, I received my first flying time in a B-25, for four hours at night. I flew as copilot for 1 hour 20 minutes and spent the rest of the time taking the machine gun apart in the nose of the plane, experimenting with the gun turret in the rear, or tinkering with the liaison radio set, trying to get Fred Allen, a popular radio comedian of that day. The ship seemed like a six-room castle. I observed that the pilot must not concentrate only on what he sees ahead, but consider the crew in the back of the plane whose lives were dependent upon the pilot doing the right thing.

On November 16th I was alert officer, requiring that I inspect the guard and attend the enlisted men's reveille. Guard duty was probably the most disagreeable job in the Army. We were tired, the nights bitter cold, the guns heavy, and the job monotonous and boring.

Back to the B-25, I would spend all afternoon inspecting an entire airplane, trying to name every part and understand its function and operation. In those early days, I didn't understand the radio and electrical systems, but having to get the information on my own made it challenging.

Our group had been at Greenville for 10 days and the earlier crews were still using our ships regularly on cross-country flights and other training they needed, so we continued to get very little flying. In the morning I shot three games of skeet and then had a blindfold cockpit check. I read some more technical material, went to ground school, and at night spent time in the Link Trainer. Some fellows were pretty eager and some not so eager. I was one of the eager ones, convinced it would be a terrible disappointment to end up as a copilot after all my work.

Finally I flew in daylight with Lt. Kempster. Part of the time we hedge-hopped. The trees and telephone poles seemed higher than they were in California. Indeed, several times the tree tops were higher than we were. One woman came running out of her house and threw her arms up in horror at the sight of our big bomber, shooting toward her house at 250 miles per hour. Once I swore we passed our wing tip through the foliage of a tree, but evidently the wing was not as long as I imagined it to be. It was dangerous but good experience.

On gas mask day we had to carry the mask all day long and wear it when we were outside or in a car, from 9:30 to 11:30 am. That was a pain but it had to be done.

The afternoon went much better. I spent time at the Link Trainer, practicing instrument let downs and some "radio range beam" procedures.

I then did something out of our normal routine; I flew as copilot to Pope Field, North Carolina, to deliver serum to people leaving for overseas duty. We hit all our check points perfectly on that trip. Two chaplains rode with us as passengers—both first lieutenants. We practically hedge-hopped all the way home. In the evening, Lt. Kempster checked me out as a copilot. Those were very busy days.

Finally, I got to fly in the pilot's seat and attempt a few landings. The B-25 seemed simple enough to fly. One quality impressed me particularly, its emergency systems and safety devices. *A lot of shooting would be required to bring one down*, I thought.

I wondered about the copilot position. Some people argued that a copilot was unneeded in a B-25, but over the following months I found a copilot was mighty handy to have. Some flights were quite long and the pilot would be exhausted. In combat, our squadron tried flying without a copilot, taking the position of "Why risk another pilot?" But they found too many things could happen at once. We really needed the extra set of eyes and hands and, of course, if the pilot were incapacitated, someone to bring the rest of the crew back to safety. Actually, later in the war, the H model of the B-25 came to our squadron. It had no copilot, but a 75 mm cannon for the pilot to fire instead. Pilots had mixed opinions as to whether that was a good idea—too much for the pilot to do.

I worked on flying or studied every day from dawn until midnight, even on weekends. Most of it was very interesting, with one possible exception, the Bomb Trainer Program. When I finished with it I felt as if one headache was out of the way. As for weekends, I had little desire to spend time going into town. Staying on the base had the advantage of catching up on my sleep.

By the time I had 13 hours of flying at Greenville, we had a tragedy. Two fellows in my flight, Lts. Quast and Humphries, were killed that night. They called in to report one engine out, and on their approach to the field the plane turned into the ground. We speculated that perhaps they were unable to keep the good engine down, or perhaps they strained the good engine. It happened just at the point where landing gear and flaps are lowered. It was a sad event and reminded us of the seriousness of our activity, requiring constant attention.

On Sunday, November 22, Lt. Kempster let us sleep until 10:30. This had never happened before. Finally, the phone rang and someone needed a copilot, so I flew for 1 hour and 40 minutes. After lunch I went up again for two hours of passenger time and then 1 hour and 45 minutes of pilot time. Unfortunately, I had my "head up" that day, feeling nearly asleep while flying the plane. That was my first bad day at Greenville and hopefully the last. I had no desire to end up as a copilot and my performance that day would be the surest way to get there.

The term "head up" did not mean being alert; quite the opposite, it meant allowing one's head to be stuck up one's backside. That was a common expression during flight training.

The B-25 Mitchell medium bomber

Copilots could be useful

CHAPTER 18
Analyzing the Crash

ON RAINY DAYS WE had little or no flying, so our regular morning meeting on those days developed into a general bull session. We discussed how to prevent the trouble Quast and Humphries had that Saturday night. Their airplane was an old B-25-B, a plane whose crew chief was even afraid to ride in. Probably, the ship would not maintain its altitude on one engine after the landing gear was lowered. All those model B planes had been on patrol duty and were nearly ready for scrap by the time we used them.

My flying resumed with another of our pilots, Lt. Williams. Just as a test, we feathered one propeller and flew on the remaining single engine. The term "feathering" meant changing the angle of the propeller blades to its least resistance to the wind, causing the propellers to stop rotating when the engine was shut down. Our plane climbed well on one engine, even with flaps down, but with landing gear down it lost 500 to 800 feet per minute. *If Humphries and Quast had known that,* we reasoned, *they might still be alive.*

Three more boys in my flight were killed, bringing the number to five lost in the past nine days. Their ship exploded in mid-air. Back at the base we speculated as to what could have gone wrong to cause the explosion. The weather was cold and the B-25 had a gasoline-fed heater to help keep the crew warm. Many crew members smoked cigarettes while flying. Perhaps gasoline vapors entered the crew compartment and the first person to light up ignited the vapors. We didn't learn any more about it though.

The weather was another problem. Not only was it winter on the East Coast and starting to get cold and damp, but eastern storms often lasted for days and the base would be shut down for flying. The weather got pretty cold, but the Army gave us warm clothing to wear. The problem was, when I wore my fur-lined jacket, I found it too awkward for flying.

One day when the field was closed due to weather, Wendell Hanson was airdrome officer. A B-17 came in, so he opened up the field to let the plane land. While it was open, Lt. Williams and I gave each other an instrument ride. Each of us had trouble hitting the "cone of silence," the space directly above the transmitting station. There seemed to be a bad storm coming so we landed, thinking that could be the end of our Phase #1 work.

Rainy days did not necessarily cancel all flying, so the next day I went up for some instrument time. After a half hour we collected ice on the windshield and on the deicer boots of the wing. I called the control tower and reported it to them, whereupon they cancelled all local flying. So our trip lasted only 50 minutes. I was concerned because it had been rainy more than clear for days and at that rate we could be at Greenville for months before leaving.

On another rainy day, when flying was cancelled and no ground school scheduled, activities got so dull that Jim Hamer and I went into town to have dinner and look the town over. We bought a few records for the record player in the pilots' alert hut, being very tired of the same old songs over and over again, and then we went to a movie. The rain dumped down in torrents that night.

When the weather was bad and there was no flying, the squadron morale sunk to a low point. Nothing could keep one's mind occupied except going into town, and that was not much in Greenville. Lt. Kempster tried to cheer us up by reassuring us, "The first phase of your training might get boring but in the second phase we will really have a good time." I was fine as long as we were flying, but just sitting around made me uneasy and in a down mood.

In addition to those tragic accidents and the poor weather at Greenville, the mechanical condition of the aircraft gave us a serious problem. Jim Hamer and I were flying one day when our heater gave out and, for the last part of our flight, we nearly froze. We returned the plane to the base and took up an old B-25-B, which was quite a clunker. Nothing seemed to work in it, particularly the heater. Finally, we had to bring that ship down because, in addition, the generator was overcharging.

We were not the only ones who experienced mechanical failures. A bad case of jitters seemed to be going around. One ship made a single-engine landing. Another plane landed with one engine on fire. Another student pilot got lost and almost ran out of gas before he safely returned. I had trouble with my wing flaps. They would mysteriously "milk" themselves up after takeoff, without my moving the lever. Also, I had the closest shave ever when my plane hit some strong prop wash preparatory to landing. It took all the strength I had, and some luck, to prevent the ship from spiraling into the ground.

Lt. Kempster showed me a near stall, just enough to get the effects of a full stall of the aircraft. We flew in the overcast for a while and then shot a few landings. It was then that he checked me out as a pilot, ready to fly with Jim Hamer without an instructor. That should make us the first pilots in our flight to fly solo, but I had too much flying time in comparison with the other students. My instructor tried to keep us even, so he sent me to the Link Trainer while other men flew.

A colonel came to the base, angry with our group commander for his combat crews not having proper training. The class that followed us from Williams Field got a 10-day leave because at that time Greenville did not have the facilities or the personnel to take care of them. In our class we had 8 or 10 men to an instructor, where ideally it should have been 4 or 5. I thought, too, that word must have passed through to higher command that the airplanes we trained in were not in good mechanical condition.

So they played the old Army game of passing the buck down to the instructors. Lt. Kempster was very displeased, as he prided himself on keeping his students ahead of everyone else.

Ground school was very important to our training. We took apart machine guns and put them back together. Then we climbed into the gun turrets to get an idea of what our gunners had to face. Our lectures were quite interesting. Most of the speakers were pilots telling of their combat experiences. A man who was on the Doolittle raid told us about the raid but, since the complete story was not yet released, he held out on certain parts. Captain Solomon told us about flying in the last war. We saw a motion picture explaining "why we are fighting." It was a propaganda picture showing the enemy in its worst aspects and ourselves in all our grandeur.

I slept till noon one Sunday, then ate lunch and shot some skeet. That finished up my skeet requirements just in time because someone broke one of the trap releases. The range would be closed for a long time.

On Thanksgiving Day we dined lavishly at the officers' mess. It was truly grand, including food items that only the military could obtain in those days of rationing in the public sector.

Earlier that day, I soloed as pilot in a B-25. Herbert Barton and I took up a plane and traded off piloting and copiloting for each other. That was just three days before Barton's tragic accident, previously described. While Barton was piloting that Thanksgiving Day, we got lost, having wandered too far from our base, with visibility so poor we couldn't find it again. So we turned on the radio compass, but it was inoperative, too far from the base. We tried next to fly the radio beam, but that would have taken too much time. Finally, we were close enough that the radio compass responded and we came down safely. Having had that association with Barton, it was even more difficult when I learned of his fatal accident.

Wendell Hanson and I flew together on November 28th. Though we knew each other since the beginning in Santa Ana, we had not flown as pilots until that day. After the flight we critiqued each other's flying, as an instructor would do. The top event of the afternoon was when Wendell and I simulated a bombing attack on a railroad bridge, agreeing that we "blew it all to hell" (in our imagination).

Lt. Williams and I flew to West Palm Beach, Florida. Departing from Greenville the temperature was freezing, but down in Florida, just three hours away, it was like summer time. That was the first time a navigator went along to keep us on track. Also, it was the first time I saw Florida. On the way home we hedge-hopped over the Everglades and got a good bird's-eye view of the state. We crossed Lake Okeechobee at about 25 feet altitude, fantasizing that we were "looking for submarines."

I learned on that day that my old traveling friend Clyde Dinwiddie (See Chapter 4) graduated from Luke Field and Wes Parlee, my boyhood friend, would soon finish bombardier training in Roswell, New Mexico. It looked, too, like we would soon be fully trained and in action.

Only one or two planes remained in commission so I didn't get to fly. Several crews left the base, probably bound for North Africa. Those who left were expected to go months earlier, but further training held them up. They buzzed Greenville in low formation when they left. Our group was expected to go next but we had no word on when.

One day I was flying with Jim Hamer for practice in blind flying on instruments. While we were away, unknown to me, the field at Greenville closed due to bad weather and all the ships were called in. We did not hear the call because our radio was tuned to the Spartanburg radio range. After four hours, I noticed snow on the ground and suggested to Jim that we go back to the base. When in radio range of the tower, we could hear it calling us. They heaved a great sigh of relief when we answered, opening up the field to let us land. My instructor told us to bend over and he gave us each a swift kick, considering the whole thing forgotten.

Sometimes my flying was not up to par. One night, the first ship I tried had an engine cutting out; instead I took up an old B-25-B model. Its engines didn't run very well either. I took up a third ship. It ran all right but I just had a difficult time with it. That happened when too much time elapsed since my previous night flying.

Lt. Dennison gave me an instrument ride and told me next time I would get a check ride for an instrument rating.

Jim Hamer and I missed dinner that night because we saw an idle airplane sitting out on the ramp and it was the best part of the day for flying, so we took it up.

A few days later Jim was having trouble with a wisdom tooth. His mouth was swollen, so he went to the dentist. The dentist pulled the wrong tooth, but Jim said it felt better and that's all that mattered. He called up his folks on the telephone, which must have given them quite a surprise and it staggered Jim financially. Telephone calls were expensive at that time. We depended mostly on letter writing to keep the folks back home informed.

My flight was planning to throw a Christmas party for some poor kids that lived near the BOQ We went into the woods and chopped down a nice tree, figuring it would look really good when fully trimmed. Then we rode to town and bought some Christmas presents for the kids and had lots of fun doing it. Fifteen of us second lieutenants swarmed into the already crowded stores. One lady commented, "I thought the Army was short of officers until I saw you all at one time."

The party for the children was quite successful. The Christmas tree was beautiful and the kids seemed pleased to have Santa Claus bring them so many things. Sometimes Santa guessed at the wrong size but generally he got it about right. The party cost each of us about $8.00 but was well worth it. Christmas in the Army during war time is not much, but this one was special.

Christmas Day! The field was closed, not only because of Christmas but also due to bad weather.

I rode in the back end of the airplane the next morning in order to get some turret time. Those turrets were complicated, requiring special training for the gunners. I wondered how effective they would be against attacking aircraft. *What would it be like if I had chosen to go to a fighter school instead of to twin engine bombers? Who knows whether I even had a choice?* The Air Corps seemed to be sending trained airmen wherever they had the greatest need at the time. Sometimes I thought I would like a P-38 fighter plane. Perhaps that was because "The grass grows greener on the other side of the fence." I concluded that the B-25 we flew was just fine.

The squadron lost two B-25s and crews at Greenville.

Sputtering engines were a common occurrence.

The weather was a serious problem, as well

CHAPTER 19
Target Practice

LOOKING BACK ON WORLD War II and the terrible destruction caused by the bombing of cities, I must emphasize that the mission of the B-25 medium bomber in the China-Burma-India Theater was not to attack population centers but rather non-civilian targets such as bridges, airfields, and ships used by the enemy to move its supplies. Even in the exuberance of youth, we looked upon our task in a serious and responsible manner.

The past several months of training lead to practicing bombing missions. That is what the B-25 was designed to do and the Army provided the Union Bombing Range for us to get that training.

My first such experience was when Jim Hamer and I spent an afternoon taking bombardiers out to drop live bombs on the range. Making runs with actual bombs was something new for us. Two bombardiers were situated in the nose of the plane, one dropping and one observing. The engineer watched through the drift meter and a third bombardier watched from the tail observer's station.

The D-8 bomb sight they used wasn't the best, especially for bombardiers who had been trained on the Norden sight, but it was good enough at low altitudes and generally used on medium bombers.

Something new was on our schedule, night bombing. At first I thought it would be as difficult as the night formation flying we did in Basic Flying School. This was my first solo night flight in a B-25 (without an instructor). I flew there with a crew of five and a load of bombs to hit a target I had not seen before at night. But the flight went as smoothly as though it were daylight.

On another day, Wendell Hanson, Vernon Fischer, and I went into town to have our pictures taken, recognizing the importance of having a record of our Army life. We returned to the base and after dinner I flew another practice mission. It was a beautiful night; a light ground fog covered about half of the ground, making ideal practice conditions. The bright moonlight reflected against the ground fog and lent a radiant splendor to the air. When we returned to the base I was barely able to land through the fog, and got down just in time.

Even the pilots were trained to drop bombs. My first five tries were not so good, two of them landing 50 feet outside the 300 foot ring, but the last one was right on a shack. Was it dumb luck?

Another activity came along. Lt. Kempster gave his men two airplanes and told us, "Keep these airplanes out as many days as you want in order to finish up your work in Phase #1 of your training." So with an instructor pilot, two bombardier-navigators, three pilots, and an engineer in each plane we started out. First, we stopped at Atlanta to repair a burned-out inverter. Next, we stopped at Columbus, Georgia, had dinner, and continued on to Montgomery, Alabama, and then Tallahassee, Florida, and finally to Savannah, Georgia. Our navigators got lost near Savannah and we found ourselves over the Atlantic Ocean, but the radio compass saved us.

After a good night's sleep in the Savannah BOQ we flew to Myrtle Beach, South Carolina, and shot at gunnery targets. When we left Myrtle Beach that night our right engine was running rough, as it had on the previous takeoff. So, we headed for Greenville but took a roundabout route to log another four and a half hours of flight time. In spite of the mishaps, we considered the trip a success. We got in a lot of gunnery and navigation practice along with strange-field landings.

The next day I observed that the plane we flew on the trip was having its spark plugs changed. Evidently, the mechanics found the cause of our problem the night before. In hindsight we might have been smarter to not fly the plane that night, as we knew the engine was running poorly. Oh well, it turned out OK! Lt. Kempster told us we might continue our trip in a day or two to complete our work on Phase #1, but we did not get the opportunity.

It was time to make up the crews and begin Phase #2 of our work which was flying as full crews. We expected that, by early January, quite a number of us would be leaving and my crew could be on the list. That was just a rumor. We could be held at Greenville for other one or two months, as happened to the previous group. Actually, we didn't leave Greenville until March 3, 1943.

I heard a disappointing rumor that my instructor planned to make me a copilot. It could have been just a bluff or possibly my flying actually had gone bad. Did I work myself into a rut? By then I had 94 hours at Greenville, which was more than anybody else in our flight in the first phase. I knew that a fellow could not afford to let himself get in a rut.

On December 28th the crew lists were posted on the bulletin board. Unfortunately, the rumor was correct—I was listed as a copilot, very disappointing news. My much greater flying time in comparison with the other men left me no reason to believe I did not stand in the upper part of the class. My roommate Jim Hamer was also listed as a copilot. He said he was going to get out of there and fly P-38s, but I told him I planned to stick with B-25s and try to get into the pilot's seat by showing my instructor that I could handle it as well as any other pilot.

The next day they changed some of the crews around and in doing so, I got a new pilot, which was a break for me. The pilot I was first assigned to was too nervous and fidgety for his crew to gain confidence in him. I even feared for the man's life.

December 31st marked the close of the most interesting year of my life up to that time. One year before, everyone was fired up about the war, not knowing what was to come. I certainly didn't know I'd be flying, particularly a big airplane like a B-25, although I knew that was what I wanted to do if the opportunity arose. That chance did come and I benefited from some great experiences and superior training. Some people would say the war would be over before another year passed but I couldn't quite see it.

Soon after the first of the year I was assigned a crew, and I was designated the pilot. Jim Hamer was promoted to pilot as well. Evidently our perseverance paid off. We continued our training at Greenville until March 3, 1943.

In January I logged 21 days of flying, concentrating on navigation and more practice bomb runs. Continuing into February I flew another 22 days, adding formation flying and seventeen more cross-country flights. February 10th was a special day, a cross country trip to Miami, then to Key West, to Tampa, and back to Greenville. Imagine the beauty of flying down the Florida Keys, observing the blue waters and white sandy beaches.

So far, I had logged 498 hours of training time, comprised of:

60 hours at Primary Flying School
80 hours at Basic Flying School
77 hours at Advanced Flying School
281 hours of operational training in the B-25

When we completed our work at Greenville on March 3, 1943, our group went to West Palm Beach, Florida, to await our assignment overseas. My crew was comprised of:

2nd Lt. David K. Hayward, Pilot
2nd Lt. Thomas T. Dunham, Copilot
Sgt. Anthony R. Mercep, Bombardier-Navigator
Sgt. Wilber G. Pritt, Engineer-Gunner
S/Sgt. George G. Scearce, Jr., Radio-Gunner
Sgt. Thomas P. Zera, Gunner

On the practice range it was "Bombs Away."

Dave Hayward felt rewarded to be the pilot of his crew.

CHAPTER 20
On the Way to the CBI

ON A COLD, DRIZZLY, early spring day I received my military orders:

> West Palm Beach, Florida. March 4, 1943. The following named officers and enlisted men are relieved from attachment to Transient Detail, Morrison Field, Florida and from all duties and assignments at this station and are transferred in grade and rating to New Delhi, India, for assignment to the Tenth Air Force. They will proceed to New Delhi, India by rail, military, or commercial aircraft, transport or commercial steamship, reporting on arrival thereat to the Commanding General thereof for duty for PCS."

I was in a group of eight B-25 replacement crews who trained at Greenville and were thereby assigned to the China-Burma-India Theater of war.

The Army provided a nice hotel in Miami where we stayed a week waiting for transportation overseas. Pretty nice duty! Medical staff gave each man a final physical exam, but it seemed not much more than feeling my pulse, as I was committed to overseas service by then.

Two officers in our travel group, Wendell Hanson and Steve Stankiewicz, were excellent story tellers. Wendell described our departure:

We prepared for our royal flyaway with a series of parties while hundreds of officers and men waited for arrangements to be made to transfer them overseas. Our eight crews accounted for 48 of them. Captain Taffy, my Cocker Spaniel, made it 49.

At the end of our 7-day "party" we climbed aboard a bus for West Palm Beach and departure at Morrison Field, now West Palm Beach Municipal Airport. We boarded a four-engine DC-4 commercial passenger plane and flew to Borenquin Field, Puerto Rico. That evening we checked the bar drinks. Large Cokes were a nickel and a double Scotch on the rocks priced out at ten cents. I limited my crew to one drink because we were going to see the world, including countries that we might otherwise only read about. I didn't win any popularity polls but my crew officers said it turned out to be a good idea.

Steve Stankiewicz, who was the bombardier-navigator on Elmer "Tommy" Thompson's crew, described it like this:

Mike Russell (our copilot) and I were the last two to enter the cavernous interior of the commercial plane that was parked on the apron at Morrison Field. The plane was manned by civilian airline pilots and they were to take us into the unknown—deliver us to the ultimate adventure of our lives: WAR.

Mike and I paused at the top step and looked back on the country of our birth for one last indelible impression to carry in our minds in the months to come. It was with mixed emotions that we did so. Our feelings ran the gamut of regret, sorrow, and over powering nostalgia. "Mike, let's take one last look because only God knows when we shall see this again," I said to him. Mike was brusque and clearing his throat. He only said, "Come on, Steve," and ducked into the cavernous interior. It would be well over a year before we saw Florida or home again.

The trip itself was an adventure. Our first real grasp of what we were in for was when we landed in Georgetown, British Guiana, for food and refueling. As we left our plane on the way to the mess hall, several RAF (Royal Air Force) fighter planes were roaring off the runway, headed out to sea. When we inquired about them we were told that an enemy submarine was sighted off the coast. I remember thinking, *A lot of good that will do. I didn't see any bombs under the Spitfires' wings or fuselages, and machine guns alone wouldn't do much damage to a sub.*

Several events stand out in my memory during that 20 day trip from West Palm Beach, Florida, to Chakulia, India. At Natal, Brazil, we swam in warm tropical waters on a beautiful beach. That part was pleasant. The down side was that I stepped on a sharp object that remained in my foot for years afterward. Natal is at the most easterly tip of Brazil, the jumping off place for the long flight across the South Atlantic Ocean.

At each stop along the route to India I heard returning airmen telling us something like, "If you think conditions are bad here, just wait until you get to the next stop. You ain't seen nothin' yet." By the time I arrived in India, I was conditioned for anything that could happen.

How well I remember the Short Snorters. The tradition was started by Alaskan Bush flyers in the 1920s and it spread through military and commercial aviation. During World War II flight crews signed a dollar bill and called it a Short Snorter to convey good luck while crossing the Atlantic. Failure to produce one's

Short Snorter upon request would obligate the person to buy drinks.

Fortunately, the British installed a refueling facility for large planes at Ascension Island, so pitifully small in that vast blue-green expanse of Atlantic Ocean. Even though our crew did not have to navigate our way in a B-25 to that tiny spot, I breathed a sigh of relief when I stepped out of our transport plane on solid ground.

Ascension Island brings back memories: walking along the rocky island shore, observing flesh-eating Parana fish swarming in warm, tropical water just waiting for food (perhaps a drowning airman?), sitting on a barren hillside in the evening watching a very old movie, exploring the British Officers Club where not a soul was present, and taking the liberty of snatching a cold drink from their supply. Belatedly, I now say, "Thank you—God save the King!"

A roommate of mine in 1944 served on Ascension Island. At times he got a little confused and admitted, "Everyone who served on Ascension Island became a little crazy."

Wendell Hanson described his memory of the island this way:

In the middle of the Atlantic Ocean lay Ascension Island (UK), the tip of a centuries-old volcano with barely enough room for six aircraft and a single short runway for take-off and landing. We could never fly B-25s across the South Atlantic without this small airport. At the end of the runway there was a 200 foot drop into the South Atlantic and the sharks were waiting. There was no chance of rescue or survival if you did not have proper air speed on take-off. On that cinder-top volcano some travelers just had time to use the latrine and it was "gas up and go." Soldiers stationed there should get a special medal.

After crossing the South Atlantic successfully, we were relieved to see the heavily forested, tropical, African coast at Accra, Gold Coast (now Ghana). Unlike many third world countries, the main street was lined with substantial stone, Georgian style buildings, reflecting the years of British rule. Naturally, we wanted to do something fun. What better way than to let the natives take us out through the surf in one of their small open boats? All went well until an extra strong wave swamped the boat. Then we got out and pushed, glad to be wearing swimming trunks.

Then, in Maiduguri, Nigeria, two events stand in my memory. Approaching the airport, the countryside seemed waiting for us to organize a safari. So half a dozen of us armed ourselves with pith helmets and rifles and set out looking for game (but not very seriously). Fortunately we saw none, but now can proudly say we went on a safari on a savannah in the deepest part of Africa.

The second event was, all through that night, I heard the rhythm of beating drums. It was eerie. What kind of ceremony could cause non-stop drumming all night long? Perhaps they were celebrating the arrival of us "rich" Americans, hoping we would leave some of our treasure with them.

Flying on to Khartoum, Sudan, I had another unusual experience. It happened in the PX (Post Exchange). While leaning over a show case of jewelry, I looked to my side and who should I see but Ray Cole, who for years was my next door neighbor on Orange Grove Avenue in Pasadena. He told me he was the Pan American navigator on our very plane.

You can guess where I was the next day. While we flew down the narrow Red Sea on our way to Aden, Yemen, I was in the navigator's compartment watching Ray take sun shots, telling me the elements of celestial navigation.

Ray explained that, on a clear night, he could triangulate his position by shooting at three stars with his octant and thereby get a reasonably precise location, accurate to within 30 miles. In the daytime, however, with only a single reference point in the sky, the sun, he could plot only a line, along which we were located. Fortunately, in the daytime, he also had visual observation of the earth below.

The port of Aden, in present-day Yemen, is rich in history, dating back to the 5th and 7th century BC as an important harbor. In 1838 the Sultan of that region deeded Aden to the British, who used it as an important coaling station along its route to India.

It was an important stop for us, too, hot in the desert sun but relaxing over a bottle of warm British beer. I drank it from a liter bottle and enjoyed it immensely.

Looking ahead to the next lap of our journey, we could not fly over Saudi Arabia but had to skirt the peninsula just offshore. Wendell Hanson commented:

Officers at Aden stressed the danger along the 1,000 mile south coast of Arabia. There was absolutely no way to help any crew that had to ditch their plane. The natives were restless, like sharks, we were told.

Our Pan American DC-4 dropped us off at Karachi, India (now Pakistan). What a change of scenery: intriguing and humid, throngs of people, strange smells in the air, very noisy, sacred cows among the people, snake charmers in the streets, and British and American troops everywhere.

After seven days we climbed aboard a C-47 transport plane and flew easterly to Agra, India. Of course our group made a dash for the famous Taj Mahal. It was completed in the year 1653 by Mogul Emperor Shah Jahan in memory of his third wife Mumtaz Mahal. Experts have called it an architectural marvel, a jewel museum of art and most impressive. But we had to overlook one thing, scaffolding the British placed around the main dome to protect it from air raids.

Agra is where Wendell Hanson lost his Cocker Spaniel, as I mentioned in Chapter 10. He was very careful about loading Captain Taffy aboard our plane each time but at Agra, Captain Taffy (perhaps he was promoted to Major by that time) was missing and never seen again by any of us.

The next day we were off to Chakulia, India, 100 miles west of Calcutta, arriving on March 30, 1943. That would be our home until January 1944. Six of the eight replacement crews in our travel group were assigned to the 22nd Bomb Squadron while the other two crews went to our sister squadron, the 491st Bomb Squadron, also based at Chakulia. The pilots of our six crews in the 22nd Bomb Squadron were: 2nd Lieutenants Elmer C. Thompson and Wendell H. Hanson, Flight Officer Thomas J. Smith, Jr., and 2nd Lieutenants Wayne M. Craven, James J. Hamer and David K. Hayward.

The Short Snorter

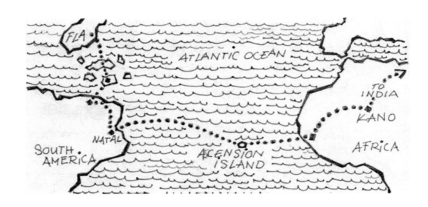

Ascension Island in mid-Atlantic

Welcome to the China-Burma-India Theater

David Hayward at the Taj Mahal in Agra, India

CHAPTER 21
Settling In at Chakulia

THE 22ND BOMB SQUADRON was part of the 341st Bomb Group of the 10th Air Force in India. When the squadron, later on, moved to Yangkai, China, in January 1944, it retained the same squadron and group designation, but found itself in the 14th Air Force, the Flying Tigers commanded by General Claire Chennault.

Reporting for duty with the 22nd Bomb Squadron at Chakulia, India, in March 1943, I found the squadron had been operating into central Burma since the previous December. All the flight crews prior to my arrival had flown their planes to India from the States, with the exception of the six Doolittle raiders who joined the squadron after making their historic flight to Japan on April 18, 1942, nearly a year before my arrival.

The 22nd had three sister squadrons in the 341st Bomb Group: the 11th Bomb Squadron located at Kweilin, China; the 490th at Kurmitola, India; and the 491st sharing Chakulia with us. Our six crews were replacements that the old-timers were mighty glad to see—they could now go home.

My first recollections of Chakulia were of natives building the airfield, using human power, carrying baskets of earth fill, and tamping the runways in a rhythmic tempo: "One, two, three, pause," repeated endlessly, in sharp contrast to the complexity of the Air Corps' program of training and transporting B-25 crews and support personnel to operate in far-away India.

Our quarters at Chakulia's British-built air base were modest yet comfortable: mud and bamboo walls, white washed, thatched roofs, concrete floors, and screened doorways. A four-hole latrine was located just outside, which we tried to avoid at night because of mosquitos and poisonous snakes. We slept under mosquito nets, yet half the squadron still came down with malaria. The other half, including me, went to the hospital with jaundice. Sleep was often interrupted by laughing hyenas and their early morning chorus. I thought, *Why not put a .45 caliber slug into one of them? That should break up the howling.* But, no! It would wake up the whole campground, including the commanding officer, and I would be doing guard duty for a month.

Natives roamed the premises at all hours. Women carried burdens on their heads and men worked water pumps for our showers or overhead fans in the mess hall. All seemed happy to earn their meager pay, generous by their standards. The grounds were scattered with tall trees; pretty to look at, yet providing little relief from the tropical sun. On my walks through the countryside a familiar song drifted through my head: *Mad dogs and Englishmen go out in the mid-day sun!* I must be one of them, I had to admit.

Open spaces provided for games of touch-football, a welcome break from our daily routine. Once we were treated by an executive with Tata Iron Works in nearby Jamshedpur, who invited us to his house for an afternoon of swimming and barbecue. The hamburgers he served tasted mighty nice after our routine at the mess hall.

Back at the campground, a troop of Gurkha guards, splendidly trained and outfitted by the British, passed through each afternoon, marching to a catchy tune played on a flute-like instrument. I can still hear that tune years later. When not flying—which was most of the time—we usually played cards, read, wrote letters, or slept.

Life in the CBI (China-Burma-India) was not all routine. Once a month we could climb aboard a "training flight" to Dum

Dum airport at Calcutta and enjoy a few days of leave. I remember my first impression upon entering the Grand Hotel in Calcutta. A group of British soldiers sat at the bar, singing:

> They say there's a troopship just leaving Bombay
> Bound for old Blighty's shore,
> Heavily laden with time expired men,
> Bound for the land they adore.
> There's many a blighter just finishing his time,
> There's many a bloke signing on.
> You'll get no promotion this side of the ocean
> So cheer up my lads, fook 'em all.

I'll not write out the chorus. As CBI'ers will agree, it is salty, has no respect for the enlisted grades, and is very impolite to His Majesty the King.

Over the years, the British brought civilization to India and fought many wars in the process. The song they were singing that day at the Grand Hotel, "Bless 'em All," reflected the feelings of many British servicemen over the years. That night at the bar people were drinking Dewars White Label Scotch. I tried it and joined right in.

The rooms at the Grand Hotel were just that, grand. High ceiling fans whirred all night, eliminating the need for mosquito nets like the ones we used at Chakulia. The food in Calcutta was superb by the standards of that time. We could buy Gordon's Gin and all the Scotch we wanted, by the case, to take back to the boys at Chakulia.

On the subject of alcohol, after returning from a combat mission we were given a straight shot of liquor, if we wanted it. Some of the boys didn't stop there, but most of us recognized the serious nature of our business, requiring the ultimate in physical and mental condition. Much of the stress could not be avoided, as time went on, and would challenge the emotional stability of each one of us. I tried to avoid unnecessary stress if I could.

Our names were posted for a combat mission about once per week, so the remaining time was often heavy on our hands. We played hearts, gin rummy and pinochle in between writing letters home. Sometimes I would take a Jeep ride through the countryside or just walk into the nearby native village. It was depressing to see the way the poor natives lived. At the base we listened to phonograph records and when we couldn't stand them any more we might toss them into the air and try to hit them with our .45 pistols. We took our daily showers while the sun was up because, after that, the malarial-bearing mosquitos were out in force. At night we watched old movies and then went to bed and listened to the laughing hyenas outside, hoping that during the night the mosquitos would not sting right through our netting.

One distinguished visitor dropped by Chakulia while I was there—Captain Eddie Rickenbacker. What a treat it was to hear him reflect on his World War I experiences, which were in some way similar to ours. It was nice of him, at his age, to make the effort to travel half way around the world to meet with us.

At 5:00 pm it was OK to have a drink. Some of the men could hardly wait. They gathered at the officers club in a basha similar to the ones we lived in. They played poker, shot craps, drank, told tall stories, argued, fought, laughed, complained, and listened to the BBC news on the hour. Art Lynch, who flew to India in our group, played a great Chopin on an old upright piano. Though not a good poker player, I sometimes joined in for something to do, trying all the while to minimize my losses. Some people thought the regular poker players were a clique that you should belong to if you wanted to get any favors. It was important to be known by the commanding officer and his staff of top officers. They were the ones who made decisions such as promotions and special assignments. The officers club was where those contacts could be made.

The mess sergeant tried to please but it seemed he just couldn't get away from the routine of bully beef one night and curried chicken with rice the next. The bully beef came from Australia on a reverse lend-lease arrangement. So did the butter which was so waxy it wouldn't melt in the hot Indian sun. As for the chicken curry, Wendell Hanson suggested that the turkey buzzards we saw circling overhead each day ended up as "chickens" in our curry. Man, were they tough! A layer of yellow oil atop the curry turned our stomachs further when half the squadron came down with jaundice. Anything oily or greasy was repulsive. That included, especially, the chicken curry. When the food became too bad we had an option—the native restaurant on the base. Water buffalo steaks were available but without benefit of aging and refrigeration, they were as tough as nails.

The bashas we lived in had mosquito-netted, framed beds. At night we hung our .45 caliber automatic pistols over the posts of our bed frames. Our basha was comprised of four rooms. One of my good friends, Wayne Craven, described it this way:

In the end room, nearest to the Red Cross girls, were Jim Hamer (pilot) and his copilot Bill Dempsey. In the next room were Jim Sullivan (bombardier-navigator on Bucky Fiske's crew) and Wayne Craven (pilot), then Bucky Fiske (pilot), and his copilot Art Lynch. In the last room were Dave Hayward (pilot) and his copilot Tom Dunham, farthest from the Red Cross girls but closest to the mess hall and the slit trench. By the way, a slit trench is sort of an open ditch for air raid protection. What you might have thought it was (straddle trench), was out in back, smelling at first of quick lime and later of waste oil and solvent wash, which was supposed to be a disinfectant and deodorant.

In all fairness I must say we had something better than a straddle trench. It was another basha-type structure, out back, with bench-type open holes for comfortable seating. But the rest of Wayne's description was correct.

One of my basha mates, Bucky Fiske, was a captain. The rest of us were lieutenants. When the provost marshal's position was vacated, the commanding officer decided our basha mate's captaincy should carry more responsibility, so Bucky became our new provost marshal. Soon there was a robbery of the squadron's payroll. Bucky's job was to help find the culprit and bring him to justice. British Intelligence brought in a prime suspect, a native who displayed an unusual amount of new money, but they could get no confession. We learned later that, although the native might have been involved, the robbery's real mastermind was an American, a sergeant in the base finance office.

We boys had our share of boredom and we did a lot of "belly-aching" (complaining). Finally Jim Sullivan arranged to have a fancy sign painted and installed over the entrance to our basha: The Redass Social and Athletic Club. Anyone wanting to hear our bitching was welcome to enter.

It was the job of Chaplain Thomas H. Clare to deal with attitudes of the men in the 22nd Bomb Squadron. Chaplain Clare was a psychologist by practice, not an ordained minister, which fit his assignment very well. He was loved by all. As a prolific writer, he recorded his experiences in letters written to his wife Irma, in San Marino, California. She, in turn, assembled his reports in book form and named it "Lookin' Eastward." It was published by The MacMillan Company. Irma gave the 22nd Bomb Squadron Association the right to publish parts of her book in its own book, "Eagles, Bulldogs & Tigers," some of which is quoted below:

Frequently the folks back home write to me and ask, "What kind of work does the Chaplain do in a combat outfit?" This is a hard question to answer because it is so simple: Everything you can imagine!

The Chaplain has to understand the mentality of the men who go out and do the fighting—in our case, the bombing. He must participate in their tensions, fears, anxieties, and problems if he is to win their confidence and respect.

Sometimes in my rounds of the barracks, I come across men who are sick, or think they are sick, and who can't seem to get the proper attention from the medics. More often than not, though, my visits to the barracks turn up humor rather than pathos. Old Private G.I. can be depended upon to come up with humor in the face of every situation; and even his "bitching" is usually side-splitting.

Chaplain Clare performed a much-needed service to the men at Chakulia, and later at Yangkai, China. It was with great sorrow that we learned of his tragic death. On May 25, 1944, while traveling as a passenger aboard a B-24 heavy bomber on his way from Yangkai to Chabua, India, his plane was lost over mountainous terrain and all aboard perished. I called on his wife Irma after returning to the U.S. and expressed the sadness felt by members of the squadron. She gave me an autographed copy of her book, which I treasured.

The CBI Theater offered little information on goings on elsewhere in the war zones, except from BBC news on the radio at the officers club at 6 pm each day. Our pre-mission briefings were limited to what we needed to know for that day—such as how many planes we would put in the air, what formation configuration we would fly, the bomb load, our flight altitude over the target, and enemy defenses to be expected.

Why not more openness? Probably, it was thought, we had enough on our minds just concentrating on our responsibilities and, also, if we were to be captured by the Japanese, it would be better if we lacked information to disclose. Squadron records show that, later on, the squadron intelligence section corrected that by holding weekly sessions to provide men with general information on what was going on outside our base. That was greatly appreciated.

The grounds at Chakulia, India

Poker games could be rough.

Bazaar Day in the village of Chakulia

This basha is the type of building throughout the Camp area. The theater is shown in the background.

CHAPTER 22
Flying from Chakulia

UNCLE SAM SENT US to India for a reason: to fly our B-25s against the Japanese invaders. Mission assignments were posted the night before, and I often wondered how long it took enemy spies to read the same lists—Tokyo Rose seemed to know. Yet, we heard of surprisingly little espionage. Early mornings featured a briefing by the intelligence officer who assigned our target for the day, usually a bridge, railroad facility, or supply depot. He told us how many enemy fighter aircraft to expect, and the severity of anti-aircraft fire to be expected—that always got our attention! We flew without fighter plane escort at Chakulia in those days.

Through 1943 and into January 1944, while at Chakulia, I flew 43 combat missions to enemy-held installations in Burma, aimed at protecting our Allied supply line over the Hump from India to China. On the bright side, I encountered no more enemy fighter planes after my first harrowing mission, as I described in Chapter 1. That one was enough to last me for my entire tour of duty.

I did, however, see plenty of anti-aircraft fire over the principal targets, as reported in Chapter 5. That was the enemy's most effective weapon against us and came in all forms, from large caliber shells at high altitude to automatic weapons shooting at low-level flights near the ground.

Other hazards, as well, played a troublesome role: monsoon weather with turbulent clouds and poor visibility, lack of navigational aids, mechanical problems with the aircraft, and unfortunate accidents. During 1943 our squadron lost 5 combat crews and 40 men. It was far from fun and games. When fully equipped, our squadron had 18 airplanes and about 200 men.

Combat missions into central Burma concentrated on hitting airfields, docks, rail yards, bridges, and oil fields. The B-25-C was designed to carry 3,000 pounds of bombs. How well I remember the night before a mission when the entire crew had to turn out and help load bombs. We put each bomb in a sling and cranked it into the bomb bay by hand. Generally, we carried 100 pound bombs when we were going to airfields or rail yards and 500 pound or larger bombs when the target was to be a bridge, barges, or ships.

On one of my missions we flew in at a low altitude and laid parachuted mines in the Irrawaddy River in Burma. The U.S. Navy supervised that operation. At other times we dropped propaganda leaflets, trying to convince the Burmese to resist their Japanese invaders.

In an early mission while I flew as copilot for a combat-experienced pilot, Lt. Patrick Ham, we had a special assignment to fly over the Hump to Kunming, China. Like so many crews had done before, I experienced crossing those very high mountains through solid clouds, at altitudes near our plane's stalling point, with uncertain altimeter readings and uncertain navigation, all the time praying our engines would keep running. With superchargers engaged it seemed we were flying in "low gear," putting an extra strain on the engines just when we wanted to avoid straining them any further. For most of the flight we had no place to make a forced landing and no place to go if we bailed out.

Crossing over the old Flying Tiger base at Yunnanyi, China, was like taking a breath of fresh air. We had completed the worst part of the trip. The Yunnan countryside was beautiful. About a half hour later we landed at Kunming, fulfilling a dream I had since first arriving in India, wanting to see China.

Returning to India and having flown eight combat missions by then, I was scheduled to fly as pilot, but not with the original crew that had come with me to India. Our copilot, crew chief, and gunner were no longer with me.

As for my copilot, Tom Dunham, late in the afternoon of July 25, 1943, while our crews were still split, an urgent call came for three B-25s to go after what was described as a Japanese freighter in the Bay of Bengal, near Chittagong, India. A flight of three B-25s was instructed to slip in undetected at dusk and low altitude, hoping for the element of surprise, and attack the freighter. Wilmer McDowell and my friend Jim Hamer were pilot and copilot in the lead ship, with Phil Simonetti and Tom Dunham in the second. McDowell tells the story:

It was the summer of 1943. We had already pulled two daylight missions to central Burma, so I well remember that night—our third mission for the day. I, McDowell, as flight leader, protested against going out again as strongly as I could but to no avail. Our three crews took off late in the afternoon in search of what was reported to be a Japanese freighter heading north along the coast of Burma. I had the other two aircraft (Simonetti was on my left wing) spread out as far as they could and still stay in visual contact in order to give us a better chance of finding the target. As it turned out, the vessel was head on. We had just enough daylight left to make one bomb run and then pull up steeply to clear the Burma mountain range that followed the coast line. I thought the sun had come up just after we started our bomb run. The vessel we were attacking was a cruiser class Japanese vessel with considerably more fire power than any freighter, and it did light up the sky.

The following is speculation as to what happened to Phil Simonetti's plane and crew. I believe Phil saw the fireworks and made a bombing pass right behind us and took fatal hits. The crew of the third aircraft reported that they never saw a thing and they returned to our base at Chakulia, landing about thirty minutes after our return. Subsequent missions to that area never turned up any evidence of Simonetti's plane or the cruiser, nor did any of our intelligence gathering apparatus develop any information.

Years later I gave the names of Simonetti's crew to the Beijing Aviator's Association for inclusion on a memorial wall at the Anti-Japanese Memorial in Nanking (Nanjing), China. Dedication of the memorial was in September 1995.

I mourned the loss, particularly of my original copilot Tom Dunham, who left a wife back home. My original gunner, Tom Zera, died on a raid over Naba Junction in central Burma while flying with another crew. His plane was caught in a burst of antiaircraft fire and went down with the loss of all aboard.

Next, my original crew chief, Wilber Pritt, decided to leave flying status and forego the 50% flight pay that went with it to join the ground crew at Chakulia. That meant it would be more than two years instead of just one year before he could return home. I understood and respected Wilber for his decision and was glad our squadron allowed flight crews to make that change.

Our mechanics had an excellent reputation for keeping us flying and they were one of the main reasons for our success. Not once did I have a mechanical failure on a B-25 while serving overseas, which is far more than I can say for the B-25s I flew during operational training at Greenville, and never did I have to turn back from a combat mission for mechanical reasons. Our aircraft maintenance was superb.

My best friend, James J. Hamer, died on December 12, 1943. As Wilmer McDowell's copilot on that July 25th mission, it must have been a devastating experience to fly through the bomb run and have the narrow escape from the cruiser, and then to learn that the Simonetti-Dunham plane failed to return.

Soon thereafter Jim requested a transfer from the 22nd Bomb Squadron. It was granted and he was reassigned to the 22 AAF Depot Repair Station at Kharagpur, India. A few months later our squadron received the very sad news that on December 12th Jim was flying as copilot in a B-24 heavy bomber when his engines failed on takeoff and the crew was killed. I was especially saddened. Over time, experiences such as that made us reluctant to make close friendships. It was too painful when good friends were lost.

Jim and I went through training together and lived in the same basha at Chakulia. I had been to his home in Eagle Rock, California, and met his family, including his lovely sister Eleanor with whom I established a letter-writing relationship and enjoyed nice visits after I returned to the States. Jim had married the girl from Fresno, California, and they were expecting a child.

On my first mission as pilot I flew to Katha Junction in central Burma. My photos show 500 pound bombs falling toward the barges tied up at the docks and of the bombs splashing in water in the midst of barges. My next mission was to the rail yards at Thasi Junction. Photos show black smoke in the target area. We later flew to the Sagaing docks near Mandalay. That photo showed a cluster of white smoke in the dock area; nearby a bridge was down from a previous mission. Next we attacked the Japanese headquarters at Maymyo. A string of bombs was laid right through a line of buildings.

With passage of time, intelligence reports indicated fewer enemy fighters in our target areas. Some of our missions benefitted from friendly fighter support, a few P-40s, P-51s, and

P-38s. While I had no fighter escort after those single plane missions early in my tour, I did appreciate, however, that someone was benefitting from our friendly fighter planes.

We had no letup in antiaircraft fire. Enemy ground batteries were usually able to get our range and course fairly well but, fortunately for us, they were not always accurate on deflection. Still, we sweated every one of those bomb runs where we had to hold a constant speed and direction. On one mission an antiaircraft shell hit the landing gear of one of our B-25s and the brake discs fluttered down like falling leaves. Some planes were lost but usually the B-25s made it through the flak fields with little damage other than a few holes in the fuselage and wings. Those could be patched up by our ground crews, who were required to stay up all night if necessary to make repairs so the planes could fly again the next morning.

An interesting footnote pertains to security. The officers each had to take their turn serving as censors for letters written home. Whenever a writer mentioned the name of a target, we had to cut that word out of the letter. The Army was anxious to avoid any information that would aid the enemy, should it fall into their hands.

However, we were allowed to have cameras, and I took full advantage of that privilege, both on the ground and in the air. One of the officers even had an 8 mm movie camera. He took many feet of film of life at Chakulia and Yangkai, and also loaned the camera to men vacationing at exotic places such as Darjeeling, India. He even loaned the camera to air crews so they could photograph combat missions, showing target areas and the black puffs of smoke as enemy anti-aircraft fire exploded ahead of us.

One day, as I was flying a mission to central Burma, I was aware that someone was standing behind me. I turned around and saw it was our bombardier with the movie camera in his hand, aiming it out the window at the Irrawaddy River valley below.

After the war, the owner of the camera sent his films to me, 800 feet in all, and I was able to use it in producing the video "Eagles, Bulldogs & Tigers in Action," which has been one of the main publications produced by the 22nd Bomb Squadron Association.

Dave Hayward and crew after the loss of Dunham and Zera

Commanding Officer Edison C. Weatherly (center, rear, wearing a hat) explained this mission planned to hit the Mytinge bridge, near Mandalay, Burma.

The targets could be bridges or docks such as these at Sagaing, Burma, near Mandalay.

Railroad yards like this at Naba Junction, Burma,
were common targets.

Often the squadron went after barges along the
Irrawaddy River in Burma.

Occasionally leaflets were dropped to the Burmese people.

CHAPTER 23
Over the Hump to China

WELCOME NEWS ARRIVED, TELLING us our squadron was moving to China in January 1944. The squadron had been at Chakulia for 14 months and was about to move to a new country. We loaded our B-25s with men, along with much of our filing cases and other equipment, and flew over the Himalayas—the Hump separating China from India. Cargo planes transported the rest of our equipment.

On the 7th of January I flew my crew to Chabua, Assam Province, and on the following day made the flight over the Hump to Yangkai, China, about 50 miles northeast of Kunming, in Yunnan Province. Our new base was officially called the Yang Chiseh Airfield, near the village of Yangkai but we Americans just called it "Yangkai." I made four more trips across the Hump in January, bringing personnel and equipment to our new base. The 22nd and 491st Squadrons were now part of General Chennault's 14th Air Force, the Flying Tigers.

Wendell Hanson described the Hump flight as this:

Everything had to be moved by air from the province of Assam in northeast India over the "Hump" to our new base at Yangkai, China. The Hump has north-to-south mountain ridges up to 17,000 feet in altitude with deep sides dropping down to white-water rivers below. Planes flew through mountain passes, where possible at 14,000 feet and at times at their maximum rated altitude.

157

Hump pilots flying C-46 or C-47 cargo planes carried loads of our supplies over that treacherous 500 mile trip. Down drafts could suck a plane 2,000 feet in a matter of seconds. Slowly, it would regain altitude and continue on to Yangkai. Japanese Zeros flew north from Burma and occasionally shot them down. Little or no rescue was possible in that extremely rugged terrain. Hump cargo planes had a greater loss percentage than most combat groups throughout the world.

Wendell Hanson's navigator Jay Percival told of another aspect of the Hump flights:

We had to make several trips to China to get all our stuff over there. On my first trip over, I was navigating and we had our plane loaded up with lots of extra people. In the navigator's compartment there were five or six people. As we got to about 18,000 feet, we all needed oxygen. We had one oxygen mask at that station and it was supposed to be mine, but I was sharing it with all those other people, to let them have a little suck of oxygen now and then.

The pilot turned to me and said, "Jay, you look a little strange. Have you been taking any oxygen? Get on some oxygen, right away." Then he said, "How are we doing on your navigation, by the way?" I said, "Oh, everything is just fine. It's wonderful. We're doing great!"

So I got hold of the oxygen mask and took two or three long drags on it. I looked at my log book. It was just as if a two year old child had scribbled and made lines up and down the page. It made no sense, whatsoever. At that moment I didn't know where we were. Not only that, but the weather below was cloudy. It was a very cloudy day.

I took the map out and saw on it the Mekong River, which later flows down into Viet Nam. At the portion of the river shown on the map, there is a big horseshoe bend, which I just guessed is about where we should be. I looked out the window and, sure enough, there was that horseshoe bend in sight. The Good Lord was with us! So I plotted a new course, determined a new estimated time of arrival at our destination and told the pilot, "OK, everything's all right now."

Living conditions at Yangkai were much improved from our previous base at Chakulia. Our campground was nestled in a clump of trees atop Red Dust Hill, aptly named by the men for the fine, dusty soil in that part of China. There were no snakes— we didn't miss those damned Indian Kraits a bit. No more of those eye flies, either—those small gnats that flew around our eyes and ears, making a high-pitched buzzing sound. And no more laughing hyenas to keep us awake during the night.

Our quarters were in pleasant, well-constructed buildings with plaster walls and substantial roofs. We enjoyed hot showers at the end of the day and American money was the common currency. The weather at 6,000 feet elevation was cool and invigorating. We had a nice officers' club, theater, and mess hall. Sometimes Hollywood stars put on a show for us, Ann Sheridan being one of them. It was a long, long way for them to travel under not-too-pleasant conditions and we appreciated their efforts. Lt. John A. Johns, a pilot and artist with our squadron, painted a likeness of Ann Sheridan on the nose of one our B-25s on the day she visited.

Limited transportation facilities over the Hump led to some supply challenges. Our Jeeps ran on blended fuel using Chinese-manufactured alcohol to reduce the need for gasoline. Cars and trucks coughed and snorted with vapor lock—but it sure beat walking. Joe Buchwald in the transportation section described it this way:

> We ran all of our vehicles on alcohol, wood alcohol that was made in China. I imagine that the Chinese were "putting it to us." It wasn't even good 100 proof; they'd water it down. To drive those Jeeps we'd pull the choke all the way out. They got about 40% power. When you were going through the mountains and the sun would hit down on the vehicle it would vaporize the alcohol. Between the heat and altitude, the alcohol vaporizes and you get vapor lock.
>
> There was a little tank up there with a bolt on top of it. To get around the vapor lock we would unscrew the bolt and put a wing nut on top of it. When you got a vapor lock you could unscrew it, put your mouth on there, and blow until your ears popped. It would force the air back into the gas tank so the fuel pump would get the fuel. You could do that, put your finger on it and screw it back in. Yankee ingenuity!

Trains and buses in China ran on coal or charcoal. The 100 octane gasoline for our B-25s had to be flown over the Hump in 55 gallon drums, by the Air Transport Command.

Our mess sergeant relied on locally available food, usually chicken and rice or sometimes water buffalo, as tough as we experienced in India. China, too, lacked facilities to age or refrigerate meat.

American personnel had to be held to a minimum, due to the supply problem. Chinese guards protected our airplanes and

Chinese cooked our food, mended our clothes, and cleaned our living quarters as well. One of the cooks, while making pancakes one day, confused flour with rat poison, sending some of our men to the hospital and many more to the toilets.

Yangkai is in hilly country, over a mile high. The few trees were generally limited to our living area. I was told the Chinese had been cutting down trees for centuries to make charcoal, a basic fuel and industry in China.

General Chennault came to Yangkai to welcome us one day. I remember his visit well. He wore a leather Air Corps jacket and his face appeared worn and leathery to match. His message was clear: "You airmen are in China as guests of the Chinese people to help them drive the Japanese from their country. You are not to fraternize with Chinese women, as they consider it disgraceful to be familiar with American men."

The General presented the Philharmonic Orchestra of Free China, who played for us. Frankly they were not as good as the Boston Pops but the best Free China had to offer and we appreciated the gesture.

In the winter months at Yangkai the air was usually clear and rarified, with a smell of evergreen trees in our camp area. Our food was clean and good. Starting our days with fried eggs was a treat and welcomed departure from breakfasts in India. We were glad to be in China and proudly took part in the continuing legacy started by the AVG (American Volunteer Group), the original Flying Tigers, and to be a part of General Chennault's team.

Days off were usually spent in Kunming. The city, along with Chungking, was one of the two largest cities remaining in Free China. Usually, we could hitch a ride in one of the B-25s making a trip to the Kunming airport. In the Jeep ride from the airport to the city we drove along a tree-lined road of which only three miles were paved. We were told it was the longest stretch of paved road in all of Free China.

The Chinese provided us with overnight accommodations in a walled hostel at the airport. Mattress covers (ticks, they were called) and pillow cases were filled with straw, smelling of accumulated sweat, but who cared if they were tired enough?

Strolling through the ancient, exotic streets of Kunming was interesting. The Chinese people seemed relatively well dressed, many of them wearing top coats when they were out on the streets in the evening. Shops carried all kinds of hard-to-get items such as automobile head gaskets, tires, batteries, musical instruments, etc.—unbelievable for wartime China. The Burma Road had been closed for months and the only recognized supply route was by transport plane over the Hump. I wondered, *Where could all this stuff possibly have come from?*

We Americans mixed right in with the Chinese people in the crowded streets of Kunming, as we proudly wore our leather jackets with the Chinese flag on the back. It was said the Japanese offered a reward for any American airman who was turned over to them. They paid the highest amount for pilots, we were told. In hindsight I should have been more concerned, but I heard no word of any kidnapping of our armed forces.

Kunming offered relatively good food and atmosphere in its restaurants. I recall visiting a restaurant and ordering dinner with a bottle of wine. It was a local wine made from some kind of berry, not grapes. That night my stomach burned something awful. Although the food was tasty, I couldn't say much for the wine.

*The living area at Yangkai, among trees
atop Red Dust Hill*

*(L to R) Rear: David Hayward, Jim Sullivan, Art Lynch and
unidentified airman; front: Stanley Schwartz, two unidentified
airmen and Tom Bullard*

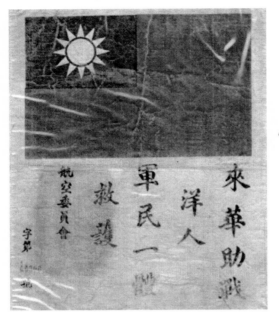

Air crews wore this flag on their jackets, asking Chinese to help return them to their base if forced down.

Actress Ann Sheridan paid a visit. Pilot John A. Johns painted her image on a B-25, in her honor.

CHAPTER 24
A Different Kind of Target

WHAT WE GAINED IN living conditions we paid for in more dangerous flying assignments. The nature of our combat missions in China differed from those we did in India. Early in 1944 we began sweeps over the South China Sea or to targets in French Indochina, now Vietnam, held by the Japanese. We focused on enemy transportation and supplies such as ships, railroads, bridges, sea ports, and airfields.

The new "skip bombing" technique, as it was called, required our planes to fly at nearly ground (or sea) level, increasing exposure to enemy firearms. Using that procedure we dropped bombs into the side of a ship, bridge, or storage area, using time-delayed fuses, giving us time to get away before the bombs went off. After "Bombs Away" we used our forward-firing machine guns on other enemy facilities.

On two different occasions our pilots returned with the top of a ship's mast imbedded in their aircraft. Our commanding officer flew one of those planes and his family has that wooden souvenir to this day. Making matters worse, the Japanese concentrated their fighter aircraft in the Hanoi-Hainan area, as I explain later.

Those low-level attacks were the most hazardous we experienced. The pilot not only had to fly the plane but also watch for other aircraft, both friendly and enemy, while concentrating on the target area and avoiding flying into the target. At low level the B-25s were vulnerable to enemy ground fire which could be intense. I recall a low-level mission in the Haiphong area when I was concentrating on the situation around

165

me and failed to see a levee looming in front of our plane. My copilot Chuck Weber, bless his soul, saw the levee and calmly pulled back on the controls as we gracefully zoomed over the obstruction. Thank the Good Lord for copilots.

Bombardier-navigator Steve Stankiewicz described a low altitude mission out of Yangkai that he and I were on. It was my 51st combat mission and was flown on February 17, 1944. Here is Steve's story:

We had taken off early in the morning, in a four ship formation. I was in B-2 position, with 1st Lt. Howard Feigley at the controls. B Flight leader was 1st Lt. David K. Hayward, a cool, level-headed boy from Pasadena, California. Ten minutes out we ran into bad weather, and climbed up to 13,000 feet to get on top of the overcast. Never once did we see the ground.

When we reached our ETA (estimated time of arrival), we flew two minutes beyond our DR (dead reckoning) position, and began to let down. We broke through at 2,000 feet over the water and continued down. We got down so low that we could smell the salt sea air. As we skimmed over the waves, the Chinese fishermen in their sampans looked up and waved—their faces creased in wide smiles.

After a systematic but fruitless search for Japanese boats, we headed for the coast and spied a 200 foot Jap freighter, tied up at a dock in Vinh harbor. 1st Lt. Elmer C. Thompson, A Flight leader, led the whole formation over the ship and we strafed it from stem to stern. He turned off, followed by Lt. Hayward, leaving two planes to take care of that "sitting duck." A-2, flown by Mike Russell, and B-2 (Lt. Feigley) then made a tight turn to the right to come in at the ship on its port side.

A-2 (Mike) came in at mast-high level with all of its guns blazing away, and rammed a 500 pounder into its side. Brown smoke boiled out of the center of the ship. And it listed badly. B-2 (Feigley) followed closely behind and repeated the performance. During the melee, a lone Jap machine gun chattered from the afterdeck. What damage it did we didn't find out until we landed at our home base.

A-2 (Mike) peeled off after its run and took off for home. But we, in B-2, weren't satisfied and came around for another crack at the ship. As we came in at the ship I could see that it had broken in two, and the front end was under water. The mast stuck up at a crazy angle; as we roared in, I looked up and saw the mast directly in front of me. I don't think a giant tree in the Redwood Forest of California looked any bigger to an ant than that misplaced telephone pole looked to me. I got on the interphone and screamed to the pilot, "For gosh sake, pull up." In the split second before we hit, I pictured in my mind's eye a very unsavory scene; that of Lt. Feigley climbing out of the cockpit and nonchalantly telling the crew chief, "Scrape out the bombardier's greenhouse and fill up the gas tanks, please."

But the pilot's reaction was as fast as our speed of closure; he pulled up and, as a result, we just scraped our bottom on the top of the mast. About six inches of the mast were left in the radio compartment, however, leaving a jagged hole on the underside of our fuselage. Just as we hit, Sgt. Arthur O. Routhier, the turret gunner, and S/Sgt. Lloyd J. Sleeth, the radio gunner, got on the interphone, yelling unintelligibly.

The pilot was too busy flying the ship, so I called them back and asked them to call in to me, one at a time. The radio man called and this is what I could make out of his words, which were shouted in one continuous sentence. "Sir, the tail gunner is wounded; he's not hurt bad, I don't think; wait, he's acting silly; jeez, we just hit the mast; there's a big hole in the rear; I'll go see how he is; boy, oh boy!!" plus a few unprintable.

With a little patient questioning, I found that a bullet had hit the Plexiglas beside Sgt. Charles A. Davidson, the tail gunner, cleared his head by about an inch, and then passed through the fuselage directly above him. The shattered Plexiglas sprayed his face and hands, and caused numerous minor cuts. However, it was more uncomfortable than serious, as Davidson spent the next two days in and out of the squadron dispensary, having bits of glass extracted from his skin. As the bullet left the ship, it ripped through the aluminum, and he was so close that wind whipped his hair into the hole. This is what had the boys in the rear really excited. So, what with the tail gunner's close shave and coming home with an actual piece of mast from a Jap boat, the gunners aft of the bomb bay cried, "Aye," when S/Sgt. Joe Sleeth of Arkansas City, Kansas said, "The black soil of Kansas never looked sweeter than the red dust of China does this afternoon!!!"

Getting back to the mission, we then found a railroad and followed it until we spotted a bridge. We still had three bombs left so we made a run on the bridge. On our first run the bombs wouldn't release, so Feigley racked the plane around and we made another run. Meanwhile, a Jap machine gun was firing at us from the west end of the bridge; the tracers cutting across our path could be seen plainly. I dumped our bombs in salvo on the bridge and lost no time getting out of there. I gave the pilot a heading to fly and we were off for home. On our return we were met with sober-faced men instead of the usual cheerful grins. The copilot, Lt. Robert K. Barron, in A-2 had been hit by the machine gun on the deck of that Jap freighter and died on the way to the home base. It was a sad blow to an otherwise successful mission.

That was my first low altitude mission—scare, death, and sadness. How do we feel about it? Sgt. Tony Mercep summed it up aptly for all of us when he said, "Just give me a crack at those…that's all I ask!!!"

I must add something to Steve's story. He told how Feigley and Russell finished off the Jap cargo ship and then bombed a bridge. While they were doing that, Elmer "Tommy" Thompson and I flew our planes to the secondary target, a railroad yard, and proceeded to bomb and strafe rolling stock and other facilities there. Rail transportation was very important to the Japanese, as they tried to move as much as possible of their war materials overland and avoid our submarine attacks offshore. Just the loss of one locomotive put a serious cramp in their needs. The record shows, among other things, one locomotive destroyed and another put out of commission. It happened like this:

I looked for a target in the railroad yard and spotted a freight train stopped along the track. First, I made a low level run on the train with my four forward-firing .50 caliber machine guns blazing and was surprised when I saw no physical damage to the train. Then I made another run with much the same result. Finally, our bombardier called me on the interphone and asked me to make one more run. He wanted to try his .30 caliber nose gun on the locomotive. Sure enough, he fired and we saw tracers going into the locomotive boiler and steam coming out the other side. He felt pretty good about that and I did too.

As a footnote to the Robert Barron story, his death led to the crews putting elastic tourniquets into the arms and legs of their flying suits, in case that should happen again.

The squadron had more problems as time went on. Bucky Fiske and his crew couldn't make it back from a mission and had to bail out and make the long "walk" back. Lts. Harding and Browne and crew were shot down in flames by a Zero over the Gulf of Tonkin. The squadron was shocked by yet another incident when we lost the plane of a promising West Point graduate, Captain Donald Blaha. Fortunately the crew "walked" back and years later Blaha rose to the rank of brigadier general.

In the first three months of service in China, the 22nd Bomb Squadron suffered major losses that seemed to claim their most experienced crews. We lost 12 of our 18 assigned aircraft and 38 of our good men, as follows:

> January 23, 1944. Hirsch crashed crossing the Hump
>   All were lost.
> February 3, 1944. Weatherly crash-landed. The crew
>   returned
> February 6, 1944. Kinzel's crew bailed out. The crew
>   returned.
> February 6, 1944. Willes' crew bailed out. One man
>   was lost.
> February 6, 1944. Parkhurst hit a mountain. All were
>   lost.
> February 10, 1944. Dubois crash-landed. The crew
>   returned.
> February 15, 1944. Gardner was shot down. All were
>   lost.

March 6, 1944. Hanson crash-landed. The crew
escaped.

March 13, 1944. Harding was shot down. All were lost.

March 18, 1944. Smith was shot down. All were lost.

March 26, 1944. Fiske's crew bailed out and all
returned.

April 8, 1944. Another crash-landing. One man was lost.

By that time, squadron morale was very low. We wondered who would be next. After losing those airmen and aircraft, our Chaplain, Captain Thomas H. Clare, spoke to the squadron. "Men, your survival depends on focusing on what you have to do—carrying it out as safely and efficiently as possible. You cannot afford to dwell on the losses—otherwise there will be more losses."

Evidently Chaplain Clare's message got through, because the squadron suffered no more losses for nearly a year afterward.

Attacking Van Trai railroad station, Vietnam

The Ha Trung bridge in Vietnam

Enemy aircraft burning at Chiang Mai, Thailand

This B-25 made a belly landing when its hydraulic system was shot out.

CHAPTER 25
Mission to Tourane (Da Nang)

IT WAS ONE OF my most memorable missions, taking me into Indochina and the coastal port of Tourane, later named Da Nang when it became an important U.S. base in the Vietnam war. The mission lasted 7 hours and 45 minutes, very long for a medium bomber. The official record provides the following details:

On the afternoon of February 25, 1944, at Yang Chiseh Airfield at Yangkai, eleven B-25s of the 22nd and 491st Bomb Squadrons were prepared for the longest mission yet. For me, it was my 52nd mission. Within the next month I was to learn that anyone who had completed 50 missions was eligible to return to the USA, but on that day the limit had not yet been set.

I was the pilot on B-25-C, serial number 41-13121. My copilot was 2nd Lt. Tom Marrone, from New York City; the navigator-bombardier was 1st Lieutenant Stanley Schwartz, also from New York City; the flight engineer-gunner was Sergeant Perry B. Bartlett from Midvale, Utah; the radio operator-gunner was Technical Sergeant John S. MacKenzie from Boston, Massachusetts; and the gunner was Staff Sergeant Richard W. Pandorf from Cincinnati, Ohio. Two of our planes were the B-25-H model, equipped with a 75 millimeter cannon in the nose. Three planes had 12 clusters each of 100 pound fragmentation bombs. The rest were equipped with 500 pound demolition bombs. Our plane had five 500 pound high explosive bombs and a full load of .50 and .30 caliber machine gun ammunition.

The eleven crews were briefed on what to expect. We were to take off that afternoon and fly to Nanning, about 400 miles east of Yangkai, arriving at dusk to minimize chances of being spotted on the ground by Japanese reconnaissance planes. We would top off our fuel tanks and depart early the next morning for Tourane, French Indochina (Da Nang, Vietnam). Tourane is about 500 miles south of Nanning. Our route would take us close to the Hanoi-Haiphong area on the west and Hainan Island to the east, both of which were known to harbor large numbers of Japanese fighter planes. We would have no fighter escort. En route to Tourane we would conduct a sea sweep at low altitude, looking for enemy ships in the Gulf of Tonkin. Upon arriving at Tourane, we were instructed to attack any ships we saw in the harbor, as well as warehouses and facilities along the docks and the railroad yards nearby.

On February 26th my crew was awakened early. All fuel tanks had been topped off the night before. I still remember our flight engineer, Perry Bartlett, helping the Chinese turn the hand crank, transferring fuel from 55 gallon gasoline drums to our wing tanks. Right on schedule, at 0625 hours, all eleven B-25s departed from Nanning and commenced their sea sweep south. We flew below the nine-tenths cloud cover at 1,500 feet.

Going past Haiphong I asked myself, *What would I do if all of a sudden we were jumped by a swarm of Japanese Zeros?* Two possible answers: tighten up our formation, enabling our gunners to concentrate their fire back at the Zeros, or, if we were unable to establish a tight formation, climb into the overcast and change direction, hoping to fool the enemy and continue on to our target.

At 0925 hours our formation arrived at Tourane, having, fortunately, encountered no enemy fighters. Fear remained, however, that we might have alerted them and they would be waiting for us on our way back. Similarly, we found no enemy ships during our sea sweep.

The river port town of Tourane was beautiful when viewed from tree-top level. An aerial photographer aboard one of the planes snapped excellent pictures and made them available to us after the mission. I traded my beer and cigarette rations for photos such as his.

We skip-bombed ships and barges, bombed warehouses and installations on the waterfront, and left the enemy's railroad yards in smoke and flames. We flew directly over gun emplacements, right on the deck. Our plane luckily avoided enemy ground fire. Best of all, no enemy fighter planes showed up. We found several cargo ships in the harbor at Tourane, along with warehouses and a railroad yard. As instructed, our bombardiers dropped the fragmentation bombs from 800 feet altitude and the demolition bombs with delayed fuses from 50 to 100 feet. Stanley Schwartz dropped our 500 pounders on the warehouses along the dock.

I spotted a freighter anchored just offshore and made a low-level run on it, aiming for the center structure on the ship. I pressed the button on my control wheel, letting loose four .50 caliber machine guns mounted in the nose of our plane. Our guns had been loaded so that, of every four shots, two bullets would be steel, one incendiary, and one a tracer.

This was only my second experience with low-level attacks. Prior to our squadron's assignment in China, while we were with the 10th Air Force in India, our bombing was nearly always from 8,000 to 12,000 feet altitude, but not so now. As I approached the ship at about 250 miles per hour, I saw flashes from the deck. My first thought was: *Those rascals are shooting back at us.* Then it dawned on me that, probably, I was just observing my own tracers and incendiaries hitting the steel structure of the ship.

That exciting experience was still a new one for me. Back in flight training we flew the AT-6 at ground targets on the Ajo Gunnery Range in Arizona. Later we had aerial gunnery practice with the B-25 at Myrtle Beach in South Carolina—but this time it was for real and kind of scary.

I thought it highly unlikely that our .50 caliber bullets would sink the cargo ship, and our 500 pound bombs were expended. So, I looked for a target in the railroad yard, as I had done on the mission to Vinh just nine days before, and again found rolling stock. It made a good target for finishing our attacks for the day.

In consideration of fuel consumption and the long flight back to base, we were allowed only 20 minutes over the target, so at 0945 hours the lead plane instructed us to return to base. Our flight of eleven B-25s had demolished five warehouses, one locomotive, four buildings at the railroad yard, sank a 60 foot steam launch and another fifty foot vessel and seriously damaged enemy rolling stock and dock facilities.

We were looking at a five hour flight back to Yangkai, which meant we would be in the air for a total of nearly eight hours. Our plane didn't have enough gas to make it to Yangkai, so I elected to return to Nanning, about three hours away, and take my chances on encountering no enemy fighters in the Hanoi-Haiphong area. I figured there would be gas at Nanning. Passing along Hainan Island, I turned on my radio compass to see if I could pick up enemy radio stations. The air was busy with radio communications and I visualized fighters waiting there for us.

Fortunately, we flew through the Gulf of Tonkin without incident and, on making landfall on the coast of China, we planned to continue on a northerly course for about 100 miles until we came to the Zuljiang River that ran east-west and passed through Nanning.

Stanley called to my attention that Nanning was close to where the edges of two of our maps were supposed to join together, and unfortunately there was a 30-mile unmapped area between the maps. Therefore, navigation by reference to the map was useless. So we navigated by ground observation, watching for the river, and also by dead reckoning (that is, relying on our compass heading, air speed and elapsed time). But we could easily come to the river and not know whether to turn upstream or downstream. Meanwhile our gas gauges were reading dangerously low.

I had a hunch which way we should turn but, as we had a navigator aboard, I wanted the choice to be his. Stanley said, "Turn left," and I complied. After a few minutes we should have seen Nanning below us, but we did not. I kept flipping through the gas gauges, willing to let the navigator have his way for a few precious minutes more. When I saw colonial mansions on the ground, I realized we were back in French Indochina and had better reverse our direction quickly. By then our gas gauges were alarmingly low.

Dick Pandorf, our gunner, called me on the interphone from the back of the plane. He and Perry Bartlett were getting anxious about our fuel supply, as well they should be. I told Dick we were almost back to Nanning. What a relief when we saw the airfield, where we landed safely and gassed up.

Another dread gripped me. I feared the Japanese would spot our plane on the ground and do a bit of bombing themselves. After what seemed like forever we finished refueling and took off for Yangkai and arrived after dark, the last plane to return. Our squadron mates were concerned about us.

As a postscript, many years later I had correspondence from a researcher at the University of Georgia who was studying the U.S. Air Force role in China during World War II. He reported that, prior to our raid on Tourane on February 26, 1944, the Japanese were using Tourane (Da Nang) as a major rear base, as they thought we could not reach it with our B-25s. But after our raid the Japanese decided to move their facilities all the way down to Saigon. So it looks like we did some good for the Chinese cause that day.

Pilot-artist John A. Johns illustrated
refueling at Nanning.

Other targets were found along the railroad line.

Attacking waterfront installations at Da Nang, Vietnam

That barge in the river looked like a good target.

CHAPTER 26
Those Who Didn't Make It

THANKS GO TO THE orderly room staff at Yangkai for sending the squadron's records back to the USA at the end of the war. I also need to thank the excellent record-keeping of the Archives Branch of the Air Force Historical Research Agency at Maxwell Air Force Base at Montgomery, Alabama, who put those records on CDs and made them available to persons of interest such as me. From the records I determined the names of 22nd Bomb Squadron airmen who died while serving, along with circumstances of their deaths. This list spans October 1942 through April 1944 when I left Yangkai.

October 18, 1942. En route from Dinjan, India, to Kunming, China, a B-25 piloted by Major Bob Gray had failure of both engines, resulting in a crash with the loss of all aboard. Sabotage was found. 22nd losses were:

Pfc Russell D. Jaggers
Sgt Herbert F. Cromwell

January 12, 1943. Two B-25s were in a training exercise practicing formation flying when they collided at Chakulia, India with the loss of all aboard. They were:

1st Lt Samuel C. Dickinson
2nd Lt Nicholas Marich
2nd Lt William J. Alton

2nd Lt Samuel M. White
S/Sgt Robert L. Propst
S/Sgt Vernon M. Harrison
Sgt Guy V. Horn
Sgt Jesse C. Levee
Cpl Finley H. Ganoe
Cpl Sidney S. Newsome
Pvt Anthony M. Mandello

July 25, 1943. In a sea sweep of the Bay of Bengal, India, this B-25 attacked a Japanese cruiser and did not return from the mission. Those aboard were:

2nd Lt Philip J. Simonetti
2nd Lt Thomas T. Dunham
2nd Lt Robert W. Gowell
2nd Lt. Robert N. Seaver
T/Sgt Walter C. Brown
S/Sgt Herbert Balsky
S/Sgt Peter Savich
S/Sgt John Welch, Jr.

August 3, 1943. During a low level attack on a dam at Meiktila, Burma, this B-25 was shot down by anti-aircraft fire. These men were killed in the crash:

1st Lt Charles W. Cook
1st Lt Henry J. Carlin
2nd Lt Nathan L. Hightower, Jr.
Sgt Sidney M. Blake

Two men parachuted from the plane, were captured by the Japanese, and taken to a prisoner of war camp. They were:

S/Sgt John E. Leisure, Jr.
T/Sgt John M. Boyd

Leisure died in the prison camp. Boyd survived the prison camp and the war.

September 10, 1943. During a medium altitude bombing mission to Naba Junction, Burma, this B-25 was hit by anti-aircraft fire and was lost with all aboard. They were:

1st Lt Max J. Greenstein
2nd Lt John Lemich
F/O Charles M. Weaver
S/Sgt George G. Danfield
S/Sgt William J. Watkins
Sgt Thomas P. Zera

December 12, 1943. After transfer to the 22 AAF Depot Repair Squadron at Kharagpur, India, his B-24 had engine failure and crashed on takeoff. Aboard was former 22nd Bomb Squadron member:

1st Lt James J. Hamer

January 23, 1944. While participating in the squadron's move from India to China, this B-25 crashed while crossing the Hump. All aboard were lost:

1st Lt John W. Shupe
1st Lt Melvin P. Fox
1st Lt Joseph A. Baldanza
1st Lt Neal R. McMahon
S/Sgt Albert J. Rosini

S/Sgt Frank E. Ullman
S/Sgt Robert L. Rawlings

February 6, 1944. While returning from a combat mission to Tourane (Da Nang), French Indochina (Vietnam), this B-25 lost radio contact in very bad weather and, running out of fuel, the crew was forced to bail out. All except the radio operator were successful in returning to their base at Yangkai, China. Missing and presumed dead was:

T/Sgt Everette W. Smith

February 6, 1944. While returning from a combat mission to Hainan Island, China, this B-25 was descending through clouds and struck a mountain. All were killed:

1st Lt Clarence H. Parkhurst
1st Lt Walter S. Myers
1st Lt Norman O. Hodges
S/Sgt Lee Radke
S/Sgt Henry J. Herforth
S/Sgt Floyd E. Webster

February 15, 1944. On a low-level combat mission to Dolen, French Indochina, this B-25 was shot down by enemy ground fire. All aboard were killed:

1st Lt James H. Gardner
1st Lt Charles F. Ferguson
2nd Lt Sim B. Clements
T/Sgt Alfred R. Sandini
S/Sgt Walter T. Ducette
S/Sgt Joseph Mihalichko

February 17, 1944. On a low level combat mission to Vinh, French Indochina, the copilot was struck in the leg by enemy ground fire and bled to death in spite of efforts to save him. He was:

1st Lt Robert K. Barron

March 13, 1944. On a low level mission to the Kiungshan airdrome on Hainan Island, China, this B-25 was shot down by Japanese fighter planes. All aboard were lost:

1st Lt Hampden W. Harding
2nd Lt Albert R. Browne
2nd Lt Robert R. Rymer
T/Sgt Anthony F. Deverse
S/Sgt William L. Hansen
S/Sgt Irwin H. Lawrence

March 18, 1944. On a low level combat mission to Vinh, French Indochina, this B-25 was shot down by enemy ground fire and crashed into a river. All aboard were lost:

1st Lt Thomas J. Smith
2nd Lt Robert E. Caldwell
T/Sgt Charles C. Evans
S/Sgt Walter Altman
S/Sgt Napoleon E. Plante

The above lists contain 69 names. After March 18, 1944, the squadron lost 47 more airmen, raising the total loss to 116 airmen of the 22nd Bomb Squadron.

Particularly tragic, on two separate occasions a total of 24 men were lost while flying on transport planes taking them home after they completed their tours of duty. Equally tragic, was the loss of eleven innocent men while practicing formation flying. Some of those aboard were non-combat personnel who requested to go along for the thrill of flying in a B-25.

Earlier, I mentioned my being in a group of six replacement crews that flew to India aboard a four engine commercial airliner. In those six crews of 36 men, seven did not return home. It was a terrible price to pay and a fortunate and thankful day for those of us who did make it.

The service at Chakulia for those killed in the mid-air collision

CHAPTER 27
Departing from Yangkai

"IF THE AIR FORCE would have come up with a crew rotation policy sooner," Wendell Hanson commented to me, "some of those men who perished might have had enough missions to go home."

For me, thankfully, it finally happened on March 4, 1944, just after I landed at Yangkai from my 53rd mission, when I learned about the new rule. The Air Force announced a crew rotation policy that after 50 combat missions we would be grounded and sent home on the next available transportation. Since I had 53 missions that meant me!

By that time, I had been awarded the Air Medal with Oak Leaf Cluster and the Distinguished Flying Cross for my service. I had flown 340 hours of pilot time in the China-Burma-India Theater, of which 291 hours were combat time.

But I had to wait for my turn to go home. Other men had a higher priority for one reason or another. To give me something to do while waiting, the squadron sent me to a rest camp on a lake at Yang Zong Hai, about 30 miles east of Kunming. The camp offered little to do, as it wasn't set up for activities at that time. The change of scenery, however, was beneficial and a welcome relief from combat. My most notable memory while there was when I saw a P-38 dive low over the lake, indeed a graceful sight.

I departed from Yangkai on April 2, 1944, returning to the USA aboard the same type of DC-4 (the Air Force named it a C-54) passenger aircraft and following the same route that brought

189

me to India a year earlier. After I left China I learned that the squadron received a reassuring compliment when the 341st Bomb Group was awarded a Unit Citation for its achievements: "Worthy of the gallant traditions of the American military service."

General Everett awarded David Hayward the Distinguished Flying Cross for his service in the China-Burma-India Theater in World War II.

CHAPTER 28
Leave and Reassignment

THE CITY OF MIAMI sure looked good to me when I arrived back in the USA on April 12, 1944. The flight aboard our four engine C-54 passenger plane took only ten days, much less time than the trip over. I checked in at Miami and they gave me a one-month leave before reporting to Santa Monica, California, for reassignment.

That gave me a chance to see how my father was getting along in his little house back home in Pasadena. It was truly good to see him, after wondering whether I ever would. My brother Stewart was off to his Navy assignment by that time. I observed that dad had visibly aged since I last saw him. He seemed confused, but still was able to take care of himself. The manager of his housing court looked in on him every day. His needs were simple; he could walk to a little grocery store across the street when he needed to. I checked his bank account and put in another $100, which went a long way in those days.

After spending time with my dad, I went out to see how many of my friends were still around. Not many, but it was nice to pick up the news from those who were still there. In walking the streets of Pasadena it seemed as though I had been away for a much longer time.

My most difficult visit was to the family of Jim Hamer in Eagle Rock; his mother and older brother were home. I expressed my sorrow over their loss, not only a loss to them but to me as well. They had no contact with Jim's wife other than to report that she lost the baby she was carrying. I then travelled to the San Francisco Bay area and called on Jim's sister Eleanor, who was attending

191

classes at Berkeley. We met at the famous Top of The Mark restaurant on the top floor of the Mark Hopkins Hotel on Nob Hill. How nice it was to see Eleanor again. Among other things, we talked about the tragedy of losing Jim. I told her of the fun times I had while knowing him. I think she really appreciated hearing that.

From our restaurant table we took in a spectacular view of the bay and the action there. At that time the government was making a major effort to avoid visibility of troop movements, so I was surprised to witness the passage of ships and troops sailing under the Golden Gate Bridge on their way to a war zone somewhere—the great unknown, that's for certain.

Having just experienced war myself, I wondered what those men were thinking. *Would they live to see the USA again?* I didn't even know my own future. In 1944 the war was raging in Europe and I could be called upon to fly against Japan again. As a veteran many years later, each time I hear that song: "I'll be seeing you, in all those old familiar places," I get a lump in my throat, thinking back to that scene watching the ships and troops pass under the Golden Gate Bridge on their way to war.

My 30-day leave went quickly. On May 12th, my 22nd birthday, I reported to the Air Force Relocation Center in a very nice hotel right on the beach at Santa Monica. A nice lady interviewed me. She pulled out a huge book full of possible assignments and began, "The usual assignment for returning pilots with experience such as yours is to go to the training command and be an instructor in the B-25 airplane."

I told her I would much prefer something special, some unusual and challenging assignment. After a delay while she turned more pages of her book, she announced, "I have a request for veteran pilots to join the flying staff of Air Force Headquarters in the District of Columbia. The job is primarily to fly high ranking military and civilian officials on their work assignments."

"I'll take it."

The Army Air Force let me remain at their nice hotel in Santa Monica until it was time to leave for Bolling Field and arrive twelve days later. My time off was pretty nice, swimming in the surf, tanning on the beach, and enjoying three great meals each day. At the hotel I met buddies who returned from Yangkai after me, bringing me news since I left. I would ask, "What happened to Bucky Fiske and his crew? Did they get back to base?"

Or, they would inform me, "Did you know that Colonel Taber was shot down over Indochina?" That's the way it went. Wayne Craven, with whom I flew many times, announced he was planning to be married. I met his fiancé, Lorraine, at the hotel, a very nice girl.

My bother Stewart Hayward was in the
U. S. Navy.

CHAPTER 29
The Nation's Capital

ON MAY 28, 1944, I reported to Bolling Field, District of Columbia, and remained with that assignment until the end of the war in August 1945. The base was situated on the east bank of the Potomac River, right across the river from what was then Washington National Airport, now Ronald Reagan Washington National Airport. The Navy had a similar base, Anacostia Naval Air Station, adjoining Bolling on the north. We were in full view of the nation's capital buildings. The Pentagon had been dedicated the year before.

The Commanding Officer, Colonel Robert C. Wimsett, welcomed me and explained my duties at Bolling Field. My primary job was to fly VIPs (very important persons) on their duties outside the capital. The colonel explained:

When you are not on a travel assignment, you will have a number of duties at the base. As an assistant engineering officer, you will flight-test aircraft as they come out of our sub depot maintenance. I encourage you to learn to fly every type of aircraft on the field, and there are many. Upon request from Arlington National Cemetery, you will take part in the "missing man" funeral formation flying over the cemetery. Chief of Staff George C. Marshall is now staying in North Carolina; he requires our pilots to deliver his official mail. You will take a turn doing that. You will greet incoming flights as they arrive at Bolling. We will have other assignments for you from time to time as well.

195

Bolling Field has quite a history, dating back to 1917 when, under the direction of General Billy Mitchell, it was known as The Flying Field at Anacostia. It was later named for Colonel Raynal C. Bolling, an Air Service officer who was killed in France during World War I. In 1941, it became the Army Air Force Headquarters, as it was when I served there. By 1962, fixed wing aircraft operations ceased due to congested air space around the nation's capital. Today, the runways are abandoned and converted to housing for service people.

I moved in to the bachelor officers' quarters and took my meals at the officer's club. The BOQ was situated very close to the runway of the airport but, by that time, I was conditioned to the noise and able to sleep right through it. The officer's club was indeed an adventure. It was the meeting place of officers of all ranks and from all allied nations. I would meet British and Free French officers and even the Russians. On a Saturday night, when drinks flowed freely, the Russians would do their kick dance, the Kozachok. This was a Slavic dance with a fast tempo that featured a step in which a squatting dancer kicked out each leg alternately. It was definitely a fun and cosmopolitan atmosphere.

Later, I shared an apartment off the base with the engineering officer at Bolling Field, Captain Charles Cline Peters, which required my buying a car to get around. It happened that Captain Peters knew of someone in the sub depot who had a 1937 Chevrolet for sale, not in great shape, but good enough for my needs. A problem arose though; gasoline was rationed at that time. It required an A ration card to buy gas. But somehow my roommate arranged for that too, through the sub depot people again.

My roommate Pete, as we called him, had an important role to play in my future: he told me about his engineering duties. I had been considering that field for myself. When I asked about it, he replied, "Dave, do you see that heater over there?" It was a fluted steam radiator. "Are you curious as to why it was designed in that manner?"

I replied, "Yes, I do wonder about those things."

He came back, "The designer was trying to provide the greatest possible surface area for heat to radiate from inside the heater to the room. That is why he designed the flutes that way. If you think in that way, engineering is for you." After the war I enrolled at the California Institute of Technology in Pasadena, California, and earned a Bachelor's degree in Mechanical Engineering.

But Captain Peters had a lady friend, a very nice nurse who worked at the base hospital. They soon married and I found myself looking for a new roommate. It was to be Bill Lookadoo, who also worked in the aircraft maintenance section at Bolling Field. Bill, as I mentioned earlier, served on Ascension Island and made the remark that everyone who served there was a little bit crazy. I won't say that Bill was crazy, but he was certainly interesting and a good apartment mate. It worked out well for both of us in that I was traveling a good part of the time and had a nice place to come back to. He had the place to himself much of the time, which he liked. I paid half the rent and that was fine with me.

Before the war, Bill was involved with politics in his home state of Arkansas, serving on the staff of a group promoting a certain candidate for governor. We spent many hours on that subject, talking politics and the future of the country.

My duties at Bolling required spending a lot of time reading through technical orders of the various aircraft that we had on the field, making sure I knew the stalling speed, emergency procedures, and flight characteristics of each aircraft. To perform my duty as assistant engineering officer, I was required to test-fly airplanes after they were serviced for maintenance or repairs at the sub depot. Many of the planes were assigned to particular high ranking Air Force officers in the Pentagon. The pilots jokingly concluded that, in case the airplane malfunctioned, it was better to lose a first lieutenant than a general.

I found my associates at Bolling Field to be most friendly and easy to know, particularly those with experiences that were similar to mine as B-25 pilots who had served overseas. One was a jolly fellow who had flown combat missions in the South Pacific Theater. His name escapes me now, but he had many a funny story to tell. Each of us had a narrow escape or minor accident to report from time to time, while flying out of Bolling Field; he returned one day with a cut and stitches on his face.

Another friend, Walter U. Nicholas, came from the 490th Bomb Squadron, a sister squadron to the 22nd Bomb Squadron, my squadron in India and China. I recall his name because he signed my Instrument Pilot Certificate. We had many a story in common to tell from flying similar missions in India and China.

As pilots, we were required to renew our Instrument Pilot Certificate each year and, as holders of that certificate, we were qualified to act as check pilots for each another. So Walt Nicholas was my check pilot and I was his. My certificate, in August 1945, indicates I had 1,719 hours of pilot time and that I had flown 763 hours in the previous 12 months.

Among the pilots on the flying staff at Bolling Field was one who had been a "barnstormer" in air shows. Another had been a crop duster and a few had been airline pilots, one of whom had to leave United Airlines because he was present when some other pilots were in an inappropriate drinking situation. He claimed he was not at fault. One of the former airline pilots seemed to be a dare-devil at times. He may have been working out his frustrations from when he had to be so conservative in his often-boring assignment with the airline. I sensed that the routine of airline flying could lead to complacency and accidents.

As Colonel Wimsett told me, when not occupied with flying assignments, I was to take my turn as Alert Officer meeting high ranking visitors arriving at or departing from Bolling Field. In the photo shown here I am standing in the shadow, off to the right, having met these officers on their arrival. They are (left to right) Lt. Gen. Hoyt R. Vandenberg, Commanding General of the Ninth Air Force, a tactical air force operating in England and France; Air Chief Marshall Sir Arthur Harris, Commander in Chief of the Royal Air Force Bomber Command; and Maj. Gen. Frederick Lewis Anderson, Jr., Commanding Officer of the Eighth Air Force, European Theater of Operations.

David Hayward (far right), meeting the arrival of (left to right) Lt. General Vandenberg, Air Chief Marshall Harris and Major General Anderson, at Bolling Field

Chapter 30
Flying Different Planes

DURING MY 14 MONTHS at Bolling Field I flew 14 different types of airplanes as pilot and 6 as copilot. This included the B-25 Mitchell medium bomber that I flew overseas, as well as the AT-6 trainer in Arizona, along with the very handy C-45 twin Beech passenger plane. On occasion, I flew fighter planes, too, when they required a flight test. That included the long-admired P-38 Lockheed Lightning, the P-47 Republic Thunderbolt, and the A-24 Douglas Dauntless dive bomber.

As copilot I flew mostly in the C-47 Douglas Skytrain and C-60 Lockheed Lodestar passenger planes, but, on occasion, I flew each of those planes as pilot.

Bolling Field even had an L-5 Stinson Sentinel liaison airplane that I used for practice in landings and takeoffs. With that plane, I earned a private pilot's license, intending to keep my options open. As the war came to a close, I thought it more likely I would fly a plane like that than any of the larger military aircraft.

My greatest thrill was to fly the P-38, the fighter plane with twin engines and a twin fuselage. As I roared down the runway, took off, and went into a left turn I started to "black out." That happens when a sharp maneuver causes blood to drain from the brain. I quickly corrected it by "letting off" on the tightness of my turn. The P-38 was truly smooth and stable, a delight to fly.

The P-47 Thunderbolt fighter plane was nearly an equal thrill. It had a huge radial engine that created a lot of torque on takeoff, requiring close attention to the rudder trim tab located on the left side of the pilot's seat. I was unprepared for that. As I raced down the runway for takeoff, I found the plane wanting to veer off to the right. I didn't dare take my eyes off the runway to look for the trim tab control so I just put the plane in a slight bank to the left and maintained my forward direction that way. It wasn't very good form but it got me airborne. Then, on my final approach for landing, I underestimated the rate at which the plane would drop when I cut back on the throttle. At Bolling Field, when landing from south to north, we had to fly over a small hill. I looked down and saw the ground pretty close but was able to give the plane a shot of power and the landing worked out all right. I flew the P-38 twice and the P-47 four times, finding each flight easier than the one before.

The A-24 Douglas Dauntless dive bomber was another nice airplane to fly. It seemed like a large version of the AT-6 trainer, a low wing, single engine plane that responded well to its controls. I flew that plane seven times, of which six were routine test flights. There is a story to tell, later, about the seventh time.

As I indicated above, having to fly so many different kinds of planes, all new to me and each with its own characteristics, was a challenge. Years later, when I read of pilots who had flown the Mach 3+ SR-71 reconnaissance airplane, reporting that nearly every flight presented a new experience, I thought of the new problems I had with the number of different planes I was called upon to fly.

There was the time I flew a Beechcraft C-43 on an assignment to Maryland. The C-43 was a staggered-wing biplane, meaning that its lower wing protruded further forward than its upper wing. It was a popular plane with private pilots, being of an older design dating back to 1933. I took off from Bolling and, as I approached my destination, all of my electrical equipment failed. Without radio communication, I could not call for landing instructions. The control tower sensed my problem and gave me a visual green light to land.

Upon landing I tried to figure out the cause of the problem. There it was! This older-designed airplane had a manual switch that the pilot was supposed to use to activate the electric generator before taking off. By my failure to do so, I had drained the battery, and all the electrical equipment failed. I felt pretty stupid about that.

Then there was the first time I flew the little L-5 liaison plane to practice my landings and takeoffs. Soon after takeoff I noticed the engine was running roughly. I landed and studied the problem. It was simple enough; with this airplane it was necessary to turn on the carburetor heater before taking off, to prevent carburetor icing. I never had that problem with the B-25 medium bomber. Again, I felt embarrassed.

With my brother off to the Western Pacific aboard the destroyer USS Putnam, my father needed closer attention. At Bolling Field we pilots were encouraged to fly as often as we could, to keep up our flying proficiency. I had a bold plan and went to Colonel Wimsett with it. I explained to him the problem with my father and asked if I could take one of the airplanes to California and look in on him. My first choice was the P-47, as it flew faster and would shorten the time on my long journey. Almost to my surprise the colonel replied, "You can take a plane to California, but I can't let you have one that uses 100 octane gasoline. How about picking one with 87 octane?" We settled on the A-24, a slower plane but it would do the job very nicely.

So on November 24th my crew chief and I took off from Bolling Field and landed at Mobile, Alabama, for refueling and a good night's rest. The next day we flew the second leg to El Paso, Texas, and on the third day flew on to Grand Central Air Terminal in Glendale, California. Total flying time was 12 hours and 35 minutes.

Before the war, Hollywood movies such as "Hell's Angels" were made in Glendale. Grand Central was the principal airport in the Los Angeles area, home to commercial airlines before they moved to Burbank and later to Mines Field in Inglewood, the present Los Angeles International Airport. In 1944, Grand Central had a 5,000 foot runway, used extensively by the military. It has been closed since 1959; today only three hangars remain. The runway has been dug up and replaced by a street, appropriately named Grand Central Avenue.

My visit with dad was timely but short, just two days. I had time to check up on him and add some more money to his bank account. I know he appreciated my being there.

When it came time to leave Glendale on November 29th I had a problem, the engine on my A-24 plane cut out on takeoff. I shut down the throttle and hoped the 5,000 foot runway would be long enough for me to come to a full stop. But it was not quite enough. I stopped in a barbed wire fence at the east end of the runway. The propeller cut up pieces of barbed wire which made a minor cut in my forehead, not serious, but it looked bad. One of the wings of the aircraft was damaged by a fence post.

Trying to think of what caused the engine to fail, this is what seemed reasonable to me: the A-24 was designed to run on 100 octane gasoline. For domestic use, the engine was converted to 87 octane and the manifold pressure gauge was "red lined," that is, marked so the pilot would not exceed a reduced figure. It is possible that I took my eyes off the manifold pressure gauge, concentrating on the runway ahead, and exceeded the red line on my takeoff, causing the engine to run rough on that 87 octane gasoline.

Nothing was wrong with the engine. The plane just needed a new wing and propeller. Fortunately, the Douglas plant in nearby Long Beach brought out a new wing and propeller and installed them. That gave me additional time to spend with my dad, but I would have much preferred the mishap did not happen. After a 12 day delay, I was ready to be on my way again. First, I gave the plane a 20 minute test flight and on December 12th, the crew chief and I departed for Bolling Field. This time we did the 13 hour flight in two days.

Fortunately, on my arrival to Bolling Field, nothing significant was said about my mishap at Glendale. At any other base there would be an investigation and reprimand if appropriate. But at AAF Headquarters we had much more freedom. I thought of the time Cadet Haskell ran off the end of the runway at Williams Field, yet he still graduated with pilot's wings and a commission as second lieutenant. I squeezed through this one equally well, for which I was very thankful.

From time to time, all pilots had to take a refresher course on instrument (blind) flying. My turn came and it required me to go to Bryan, Texas, to take the course. Upon its completion, the supervising officer told me I would be required (shanghaied?) to remain there as a part of their permanent staff. My jaw dropped when he said it. Fortunately, we had higher authority at AAF Headquarters than they had at Bryan and I was able to return to my job at Bolling Field.

Assignments at Bolling were varied. One of our duties as pilots was to take turns delivering official mail to General George C. Marshall who spent much of his time at the Army's Fort Bragg near Fayetteville, North Carolina. General Marshall was U. S. Army Chief of Staff and chief military advisor to President Franklin D. Roosevelt, so he had to keep in close touch with Washington.

My first trip went like this: Early in the morning I took off from Bolling Field in an AT-6 trainer and hopped across the Potomac River to Washington National Airport. A master sergeant, all "spit and polish" in his immaculate uniform, climbed into the back seat of the plane. Chained to his wrist he carried a briefcase containing official mail for the general. We flew to a grass field at Fort Bragg, the sergeant got out, and a car was waiting.

Who should step out of the car but General George C. Marshall? He walked up to me and I saluted, of course. The general asked me my name and where I served overseas. After a few pleasantries he thanked me and departed with the sergeant. I climbed back into the plane, took off for Pope Field nearby, and called a number on the telephone using priority one. After reporting my successful delivery of the general's mail I refueled the plane, had my lunch, and departed for the grass field at Fort Bragg again.

There, I picked up the sergeant with the briefcase chained to his wrist and we took off for Washington National Airport. The sergeant got out and entered a waiting car and I hopped across the Potomac to Bolling Field. That made a long and interesting day. I repeated that routine several times while stationed at Bolling, but that was the only time I had the pleasure of meeting the general face-to-face.

Another thing we pilots did at Bolling Field, when not on a tour, was fly the "missing man" formation during ceremonies at Arlington National Cemetery. At a predetermined time we would take off with 4 AT-6s and fly a V-shaped formation over the cemetery. Two planes flew on the left wing of the lead plane and only one on the right side. Our "missing man," of course, represented the loss of a person important to the war effort.

When our pilots finished the fly-by we routinely flew out where the Potomac River was wide and clear, and engaged in a mock "dog fight," as the fighter planes do in combat. It was a lot of fun but, under other circumstances, could result in a serious penalty, as low flying was generally forbidden. In this case, we could claim it was just a part of the missing man fly-by.

P-38

P-47

CHAPTER 31
Flying the VIPs

SOON AFTER ARRIVING AT Bolling Field I was assigned to fly as copilot for the Secretary of War, Henry L. Stimson. He wanted to go to Miami, Florida, for a one-week rest. The pilot of the plane was a full colonel and the plane we flew in was a specially designed C-47. The crew chief was a friendly master sergeant who traveled regularly with the secretary and knew the drill well. Upon reaching Miami, the colonel pilot told me to plan on remaining in Miami for the entire week, but be ready to bring Secretary Stimson back to Washington on short notice if necessary. That wasn't bad duty at all. How does a 22 year old young man keep busy in Miami with nothing but time on his hands, with no friends or connections in the area? Somehow, I did.

Many of my flights as pilot were with Brigadier General Patrick W. Timberlake, Deputy Chief of Air Staff, Army Air Forces. He made visits to Air Force installations throughout North America and liked the B-25 so much that he wanted to fly it himself most of the time. That was fine with me.

In June 1944, we flew to Havana, Cuba. While the general was taking care of business I explored the town. Most impressive to me was Sloppy Joe's Bar, claiming to be the "Longest Bar in the World" and made famous by Ernest Hemingway who lived in Cuba back in 1939.

The general and I next flew to Jamaica and landed at Kingston, its capital. Under terms of the "lend-lease" agreement we had with Great Britain, the U.S. established military bases on some of the islands of the Caribbean, Jamaica being one, and personnel in Washington conducted business at those bases. Kingston was tropical, hot and humid, but as we drove through the rain forests, into the higher inland region of the island, the weather became more pleasant. Arriving at the U.S. base, the general dropped me off at the officers club for rest and relaxation while he went on to make his appointments. A very polite Jamaican waiter came up to me and asked what I would like to drink. I saw someone else with a gin and tonic, an appropriate tropical drink, and ordered the same. It was most refreshing. The ambience of the club and its surroundings was indeed impressive, so different from Washington, stimulating my imagination to the limit.

When we returned to Bolling Field, the base Adjutant forwarded to me a letter General Timberlake had written to the commanding officer of Bolling, dated June 27, 1944:

> On my recent inspection trip made in a Bolling Field aircraft, I was accompanied by Lieutenant David K. Hayward and crew from your station. I wish to commend this young officer and bring to your attention the efficiency and courtesy shown to me, and the very capable manner in which he handled the aircraft and crew.

I appreciated that very much, but in my view, I was just doing my job. General Timberlake came from a family with a strong military tradition of producing West Point graduates, of which he was one. I made many flights with the general in a B-25. Sometimes he flew as pilot and at other times I did; as he had gone through the Air Corps flying school at Brooks Field, Texas, years before. We established an informal relationship. When the two of us were alone, he was Pat and I was Dave, but when other people were present we were strictly formal.

The general asked me if I intended to remain in the Air Force after the war was over. I told him I was leaning toward leaving the service and taking advantage of the GI Bill of Rights for an education in engineering. He attended the Air Corps Engineering School in 1933 and replied that the Air Force would provide an engineering education for me if I chose to make a career in the service. Wow! What an offer! And what a connection! I thought seriously about it.

In Chapter 30, Flying Different Planes, I mentioned how some flights that should be uneventful could indeed present a problem. On one such flight I was flying a C-45, returning from Texas with a high-ranking officer aboard. We were flying above an overcast, with no sight of the ground below, and our radio went out, important to our navigation.

As I touched on before in this book, in those days the pilot had three principal methods of navigating (I am not including celestial navigation). If we could see the ground, we would look for prominent features such as rivers, cities and railroads, and correlate them with our maps. We called that "pilotage." The second way was called "dead reckoning," where we flew a predetermined compass course for a predetermined length of time, knowing our airspeed, and expected to end up at our planned destination. The third and most common way was "flying the beam." Civil airways throughout the country connected the major cities. A radio beam was sent out from stations along those civil airways to guide the pilots. If he heard an N or an A in Morse code, he would know he was on one side or the other of the beam. If he heard a steady tone, he would be directly on the civil airway. Airplanes were instructed to fly at different odd-or-even thousand foot intervals to avoid collision with planes coming from the other direction. If the beam went silent, the pilot would be in the "cone of silence" directly over the transmitter, near a major airport or check point.

When my radio failed that day I was flying the beam and lost my means of navigation. I could not see the ground and dared not drop down through the overcast for fear of hitting another plane or an obstruction below. Back in India or China, when a pilot was flying above a cloud layer and lost his way, a common option was to fly as far as possible on his remaining fuel and then order all aboard to jump out in parachutes. That certainly was not what I wanted to do in this case.

It turned out that another radio set was available, but it could transmit and receive only in Morse code. I had some training in using Morse code but did not feel confident to use it at the time, along with having to fly the airplane. It happened that my passenger was very familiar with Morse code and he took over the job of contacting the ground station while I concentrated on flying the plane. Before long he gave us a heading to the nearest airport, along with weather conditions and approval to descend through the clouds. Wow! Another close call, and I felt embarrassed that I had to depend on someone else to resolve it.

My longest VIP trip, for 15 days, began in January 1945. I was copilot in a C-47 type passenger plane. The General aboard was making an inspection of all the major seaports in the Gulf of Mexico and along the Pacific Coast. The first stop was New Orleans. While the general and his staff took care of official duties I made a bee line for the French Quarter. Can you imagine the first impression of a 22 year old in a place like that? I couldn't believe it was happening. The music! The history! The ambience!

Arriving at the Pacific Coast, we stopped at Los Angeles, San Francisco, Portland, and Seattle. At Los Angeles I dropped in on my father again to see how he was getting along and put a little more money in his bank account. At San Francisco I visited with Eleanor Hamer, whom I liked a lot.

After Seattle we stopped at Prince Rupert, British Columbia. From there we took a side trip with the general, on a small boat to Ketchikan, Alaska. What a wild place it was in those days! It seemed like the last frontier. I had the impression the inhabitants' favorite form of exercise was drinking booze. They consumed plenty of it and their wildness was evidence.

While in Ketchikan, I purchased a small totem pole crafted by a local Tlingit Indian on the nearby island of Metlakatla. That totem pole now resides in the living room of my son Kirk.

We flew back to Washington by way of Edmonton, Canada, providing all of us in the plane an opportunity to buy something hard to get in the U.S.—beef, all we wanted of it. No ration card was needed in Canada.

In September 1944, I picked up a C-45 and flew Brigadier General F. A. Heileman on an inspection trip that was to go to the West Coast. He was Director of Supply, Army Service Forces. The general wanted to see the Grand Canyon on his way, so he instructed me to land at Ashfork, Arizona, about 67 miles from the canyon rim. He arranged for a car to pick him up at Ashfork and drive him to Grand Canyon.

Ashfork's airfield was known as Ashfork Intermediate Field, one of many unpaved airfields along the civil airway in the early days of commercial aviation, which were available as emergency landing fields if needed. The runway was 4,100 feet long. I looked at the wind sock to determine the wind direction and brought the C-45 in from the east. I landed and coasted for a stop, but what happened next? That 4,100 foot runway wasn't quite long enough to bring the airplane to a complete stop. I ran into a fence at the end of the airstrip. What a mess! And with a general aboard, too!

Fortunately no one was injured but the plane was damaged and the general had to change his plans.

How could that have happened? Did the wind shift just before I landed? Was it the high altitude? To this day I don't know. The C-45 had the type of landing gear that prevented me from slamming on the brakes. If I did, we might have nosed over.

Well, that was the end of my trip with General Heileman. As far as I know, he entered his awaiting car and completed his trip to Grand Canyon. I called Bolling Field to report the accident and then stayed at Ashfork until the plane was repaired, finally returning it to Bolling Field 16 days later.

On October 2nd, General Heileman sent a letter to our Commanding Officer, Colonel Wimsett, saying:

I have just completed a two-week trip with members of my staff in a C-45 transport plane, arrangements for which were made by Colonel de Rosier, Army Air Forces Liaison Officer with the Army Service Forces. The splendid cooperation of the Army Air Forces permitted me to visit many depots in the Seattle, San Francisco, Los Angeles, and Ogden areas with minimum absence from my office. The performance of the ship's crew was excellent, and in spite of a small mishap we maintained our schedule throughout.

I should therefore like to commend the pilot, Lt. D. K. Hayward, who was unfailingly courteous and efficient, and showed considerable ingenuity and ability. I wish also to commend the crew chief, Sergeant H. Luskawski. Please accept my thanks for the manner in which this mission was organized and performed, and also convey my thanks to Lt. Hayward, Sgt. Luskawski, and the others who contributed directly to our convenience.

By reading that letter it might be assumed I would not suffer any unpleasant consequence, but it did not turn out that way. I lost a promotion to captain, a sad development for me. Colonel Wimsett called me into his office. Captaincies were being awarded to first lieutenant pilots having about the same time and experience I had.

The colonel said to me, "Ordinarily I would promote you to the rank of captain, but under the circumstances of the accident at Ashfork I just can't do it. I'm sorry to have to tell you that."

I was not surprised, but terribly disappointed. After all I had been through, and with an otherwise good record, I really wanted to leave the Air Force as a captain.

My duties at Bolling Field continued into 1945 with no problems except one, ground looping an AT-6 on my return from one of the courier flights to Fort Bragg, delivering General Marshall's mail. In order to keep a heavy aircraft such as a B-25 going straight down the runway on landing, it was necessary to make short jabs on the rudder pedals. But that was definitely not the right thing to do when landing a light weight AT-6. Habits are hard to break. I did exactly that with the AT-6.

Perhaps I was getting more tired than I realized after three years of the war. Was I losing what an airplane pilot needs most, his efficiency? My allergy to east coast pollens didn't help during that hot summer in Washington, sometimes interfering with landings and takeoffs. We kept our canopies open during those operations and the rush of air into the cockpit could bring in pollens. But I was most thankful that, during those three and a half years, I survived without any serious accidents, and felt pleased and lucky about that.

General Timberlake liked to fly the B-25.

David Hayward usually flew the VIPs in the C-45 Beechcraft passenger plane. This was General Heileman's group.

CHAPTER 32
The War Was Over

AUGUST 15, 1945, WAS a great day. The war was finally over. I had flown 903 hours of pilot time while at Bolling Field, for a total of 1,742 hours flown during World War II. Included were 291 hours of combat time on 53 missions overseas. I had been in the war for three years and six months and was very relieved to see the end. Unfortunately, many of my friends did not make it through.

It was time to make decisions, whether to remain in the service and make it a career, go to work for the airlines with generous salaries for pilots, or to take advantage of the GI Bill of Rights and pick a good school for a first class education. I had worked with older pilots who faced that decision earlier in their lives. Those who had been airline pilots thought the work was often boring and led to complacency. Some had gone into barnstorming and crop dusting, not appealing to me at all. The smart ones, they advised, went back to school.

As for me, the regimented life of the military was not my style. I preferred the GI Bill of Rights and its generous offer to pay for my education at a first class engineering school.

On August 21st I received military orders from Fort Meade, Maryland, changing me to inactive status as of October 25, 1945, and to be issued a Certificate of Service. I was tendered appointment in the Officers Reserve Corps on August 21st, in the Army of the United States (AUS) for a period of five years.

On July 3, 1952, the Air Force advised me that, in view of my service as an Aviation Cadet in the AUS, I was credited with

217

more than ten years of Reserve time. They awarded me the Armed Forces Reserve Medal as of July 11, 1952. On August 25, 1952, I resigned from the Air Force Reserve to devote my attention to family life and a civilian career.

For the record, the medals and awards for my serving in the military are the following:

Distinguished Flying Cross
Air Medal with one Oak Leaf Cluster
Asiatic-Pacific Campaign Medal
Honorable Service Lapel Button WWII
Presidential Unit Citation
Good Conduct Medal—Air Force
Armed Forces Reserve Medal
World War II Commemorative
China-Burma-India 1941-1945 Commemorative
50th Anniversary of World War II Commemorative

My August 21, 1945, orders gave me one month of leave and 14 days for travel expenses. So I said goodbye to my friends at Bolling Field and packed my things in my old 1937 Chevrolet sedan. Hopeful that the car would hold together, I crossed the country and arrived safely in Pasadena, California. I drove at speeds no greater than 25 miles per hour, just to be easy on the car over the narrow two lane highways through the Appalachian Mountains, and onto the historic Route 66 and home. I made it, thanks to the Good Lord. Luck served me once again.

On arriving home I asked myself: *Why not apply to California Institute of Technology?* Caltech is what we called it, located conveniently in my home town. But could I get in? After 3 ½ years of war, how could I possibly compete with young kids fresh out of high school? I bought some high school level books on physics, math, and chemistry and crammed. Then, I took the entrance exam at Caltech and was the most surprised guy in Pasadena when they accepted me. Although I had completed two years of college at Pasadena Junior College, I started all over again as a freshman at Caltech in the fall of 1945. Other veterans like me, with similar wartime experiences, became my roommates and close friends. There was Sammy Fong, a B-24 pilot who flew over Ploeste, Romania, and George Hrebec, a B-17 pilot who survived missions over Germany, and others as well. I felt at home. We wore our Air Force leather jackets around the campus, as part of a family again.

The professors at Caltech went out of their way to give us veterans extra time, if necessary. Sophomore physics was tough for me and I took advantage of Dr. Tim Lauretsen's offer to help understand what we called "word problems" in physics. We had student houses at Caltech, similar to fraternities but without national ties. Mine was Dabney House, which I joined in my sophomore year. As one of the "older" students, 26 at the time, they elected me to serve as President of the house in my senior year.

CHAPTER 33
Wilmer McDowell—Reunions

ON AUGUST 3, 1943, Lt. Charles W. Cook and his crew were shot down on a low level attack on a dam at Meiktila, Burma. His radio operator-gunner, John M. Boyd, bailed out of the badly damaged plane but was captured quickly by the Japanese and sent to a prison of war (POW) camp in Rangoon, Burma, where he remained for the duration of the war. His survival during those two years, under unbelievable conditions, was truly miraculous. After John returned home, he arranged for a group of POWs he knew at Rangoon to meet for a reunion each year.

In 1987 John had a great idea. Why not hold a reunion of 22nd Bomb Squadron veterans? They could meet at St. Louis, Missouri, immediately following the POW reunion. So John picked up his directory of the 14th Air Force Flying Tigers and, with the help of Ted Kratzke of the 22nd, proceeded to contact all the veterans they could find. It worked. Sixty seven veterans of the 22nd met at St. Louis in 1987 and held their first reunion. John Boyd was deemed the "father" of the 22nd Bomb Squadron Association. Wilmer E. "Wil" McDowell was president and Ski Bashinski, treasurer. McDowell would play a major role in the future course of the Association.

In 1989 the veterans met in Reno, Nevada, organized by "father" John Boyd and President McDowell. Twenty seven veterans attended; family and friends raised the total to 62 persons.

Wil introduced Carl Wildner who reported on his role in the Doolittle raid on Japan, describing his training, takeoff from the

221

aircraft carrier, the bombing, crash landing, and return to friendly China. Next, Lloyd Klar told of his third mission when the crew inadvertently armed and released fragmentation bombs within the bomb bay of his airplane. Lloyd explained how the crew picked up the bombs and threw them out of the plane, through the photographer's port.

President Wil called on me to show slides of the trip my wife Jeanne and I took to mainland China earlier in 1989, comparing old China with the new. It brought back memories to more than one veteran. During the rest of the afternoon and evening our veterans renewed old friendships and told their tales while viewing photo albums and taping anecdotes of their wartime experiences, which Wil McDowell strongly encouraged.

Members elected a slate of officers for the following year: Gordon Berg as president, Bob Yeck as vice president, Tom Pratt as treasurer, David Hayward as secretary, and Forrest McElwain as sergeant at arms. Past President Wil McDowell remained on the Board of Governors. Tom Pratt turned over the job of treasurer to me and I continued in the new position of secretary-treasurer.

The 22nd Bomb Squadron Association was born. McDowell directed a group of veterans, including Chuck Weber and me, to draft a constitution and set of bylaws and to incorporate the association in the State of California.

Quoting the Association's constitution: "The purpose of the 22nd Bomb Squadron Association shall be: (A) To preserve the history, fellowship and tradition of its World War II experience; (B) To meet regularly for social, business and educational purposes; (C) To make available for posterity a record of personal experiences, including data and anecdotes."

In accordance with item (B), the association held reunions regularly in subsequent years. Frequently, a veteran would offer to host a reunion in his home town. As secretary-treasurer, I was involved in them and attended every reunion commencing with Reno in 1989. Wil McDowell planned each reunion as long as he was able to do so. He also organized a search for "lost" members and established a list of all veterans he and his team could locate. With the help of his wife Myra, Wil also created a roster of men who served in the 22nd Bomb Squadron and he saw that it was placed in the squadron's new publication "Eagles, Bulldogs & Tigers."

The Chinese planned a memorial at Nanjing to honor American airmen who made the supreme sacrifice while helping to drive the invaders out of their country. They asked Wil to provide a list of such names from the 22nd Bomb Squadron, which he did at considerable effort. Today, visitors can view stone tablets in Nanjing with familiar names of those who died in service. The Chinese built a similar stone wall in the city of Zhijiang, where the Japanese laid down their arms to the Chinese in 1945.

Wil McDowell was born in 1917, enlisted in the Army Air Corps, received his pilot training before the war, piloted one of the 26 B-25s to India in 1942 as a part of Project 157, and remained in the Air Force until retirement as lieutenant colonel.

In the year 2000, he reached the age of 82. Although failing in health, he joined our group of veterans who returned to China that year. The tour included dedication of the Hump Pilots Monument at Kunming, China. Atop a long flight of stone steps a group of Buddhist monks assembled with their objects of various fruits and symbols to make the dedication. While the rest of our group was climbing the long stairway, Wil McDowell waited below, not wanting to attempt it. But we were highly surprised and pleased, a few minutes later, to turn around and see Wil standing there with us on top of the steps. He didn't want to miss the ceremony.

Wil brought with him that year his eldest son Rupert who, along with daughter Lucy, continued the McDowell tradition of service to the 22nd Bomb Squadron Association. Lucy assisted with membership assignments and Rupert, or "Rupe" as we call him, took on the burdensome job of reunion chairman. Wilmer McDowell passed away in 2001 and was highly admired by all those who knew him.

My principal role as secretary-treasurer was to implement items (A) and (C) of the purpose of the 22nd Bomb Squadron Association, as stated in the constitution, which led to the following publications:

The book "Eagles, Bulldogs & Tigers," the squadron history containing 298 stories and 428 illustrations.

The DVD "Eagles, Bulldogs & Tigers in Action," the squadron history in video form.

The book "WWII DIARY," more stories by veterans of the squadron.

The booklet "The Bombing Bulldogs in the Salween River Campaign," on the role played by the 22nd Bomb Squadron in helping to drive the invaders out of southwest China.

The quarterly newsletter for members and supporters of the Association.

The collection of past newsletters in CD form.

The history of past reunions in DVD form.

Reunions of the 22nd Bomb Squadron

Year	Location	Attendance Veterans/Total
1989	Reno, NV	27/62
1990	Pittsburgh, PA	25/51
1991	Kansas City, MO	35/65
1992	Rapid City, SD	40/81
1993	Seattle, WA	38/94
1994	San Antonio, TX	46/115
1995	Braintree, MA	30/72
1996	The Bahamas	21/68
1997	Las Vegas, NV	42/98
1998	Dayton, OH	39/72
1999	Colorado Springs, CO	25/68
2000	Gettysburg, PA	20/64
2001	Tucson, AZ	24/63
2002	Branson, MO	20/58
2003	Oshkosh, WI	15/48
2004	New Orleans, LA	13/45
2005	Columbia, SC	13/49
2006	San Francisco, CA	11/32
2007	Omaha, NE	7/30
2008	Portland, OR	6/40
2009	Knoxville, TN	7/29
2010	Alexandria, VA	5/45
2011	San Diego, CA	3/19
2012	San Antonio, TX	3/22
2013	Savannah, GA	4/16

John Boyd, the "father" of the 22nd Bomb Squadron Association

Wilmer McDowell, the association's first president

At the 22nd Bomb Squadron reunion in Reno, Nevada, in 1989, the officers drank a toast to the future of the 22nd Bomb Squadron Association. (Left to right): Vice President Bob Yeck, Treasurer Tom Pratt, Secretary Dave Hayward, and Sergeant at Arms Forrest McElwain

Wilmer McDowell's son Rupert carries on the McDowell tradition by serving as reunion chairman.

CHAPTER 34
Return to China in 1989

AFTER THE WAR I enrolled at Caltech and earned a Bachelor of Science degree in Mechanical Engineering in June 1949. The GI Bill of Rights was paying off. At the same time, a young lady by the name of Jeanne Thompson was working on her Bachelor's degree in Mathematics at the University of California at Los Angeles. She, too, graduated in June 1949. A mutual friend at Caltech, Richard Alexander, knew us both and thought we would make a good match, so he arranged for us to meet. We met on the Fourth of July weekend following our graduation. On September 14, 1951, we were married. In the years that followed, the Good Lord gave us three fine sons. Gary was the oldest, Eric the next, and Kirk the youngest.

After our meeting in 1949, Jeanne went to work as a mathematician at Rand Corporation in Santa Monica, a research and development contractor for the U.S. government. I joined up with Texaco, reporting first to Long Beach, California. The work was in oil field development and production. At nights, I attended the University of Southern California and earned a Master's degree in Petroleum Engineering. The California GI Bill of Rights paid off that time.

I continued with Texaco for 18 years and then transferred to the California State Lands Commission, involved with development of the huge oil field in Long Beach harbor. Jeanne left Rand when we were married and then worked for North American Aviation, the same company that built the B-25s we flew in the war. After taking time out for child-raising, Jeanne went back to school and earned a teaching certification, leading to a career as an elementary school teacher. She retired in 1985 and I retired in 1990, by which time Jeanne joined with friends as a travel agent.

One of the trips Jeanne planned was the journey for us to China. The itinerary would take us to the principal attractions as well as places I knew during World War II. We landed at Beijing just as demonstrations at Tiananmen Square were happening. Then we moved to the Stone Warriors at Xian, a Yangtze River cruise, and the wartime capital of Chungking (now Chongqing). Our guide pointed out the little island in the middle of the Yangtze River where the original Flying Tigers flew from. We then flew to Kunming, familiar territory to me, and to Kweilin (now Guilin) where our sister squadron, the 11th Bomb Squadron, flew their B-25s, and on to Hong Kong before returning to Beijing and home.

The Kunming where our Chinese YUN-7 turboprop landed was vastly different from what I had left 45 years earlier. There was no sign of the old hostel at the airport. The familiar "Follow Me" Jeep to guide landing aircraft was nowhere to be found. Instead of open fields on the way to the city, there were now high rise apartments and hotels and other signs of China's emergence from its past.

As I stepped out of the plane and breathed the dry, rarified air at mile-high Kunming, my memories came back. Our drive from the airport to Kunming was along the same tree-lined road I had traveled in 1943 and 1944, the 3-mile stretch of road that was reported to be the longest paved road in all of Free China. I saw very little automobile traffic but, on either side of the road, the inevitable signs of high-rise construction.

The flashbacks continued. Walking up Wuhua Hill on Yuontong Street, I saw the same shops as before, although somewhat shabbier now. On the road to Stone Forest I saw the old rest camp on the lake at Yang Zong Hai, where I spent a week in 1944 while waiting to go home. That place was still known as the Flying Tiger rest camp, but now occupied by a unit of the People's Liberation Army.

Standing at the spot where the Burma Road began was a moving experience. A stone marker still indicated the zero kilometer point on the road. A huge sign in Chinese read: "This is street curve. Please slow down." I thought about how many more "street curves" lay ahead on the long road to Burma.

Our guide asked me why the Burma Road was of such interest to Americans. I explained that it was one of the main reasons the Americans came to China, the only route left open for supplies to China. The Flying Tigers were sent to China to defend the road, and the 14th Air Force and other units followed with the objective of getting it all back from Japanese occupation.

For every flashback to World War II there was a contrast. We swapped alcohol-burning Jeeps for air conditioned Toyota mini buses. Instead of restricted travel due to fuel shortages and flying responsibilities, we were now free to visit the Golden Temple, the Dragon Gate in the Western Hills, Daguan Pavilion, the Stone Forest, and war lord Nong Yun's villa at Green Lake Park. Rather than spending an evening at a dingy bar, we danced at the disco in the posh Golden Dragon Hotel, one of the many modern hotels in Kunming.

One thing was obviously missing at Kunming—a memorial to those of us who served there in World War II. Our guide told us that, until recent years, the Chinese people generally associated Americans with Chiang Kai Shek, but now more people realized that both Chiang and Mao were fighting for their country.

As our guide mentioned that day, the Chinese people were beginning to change their attitudes toward the Americans who helped them drive the invaders from their country back in World War II.

We departed from Kunming on May 5, 1989, in a Boeing 737. As the plane took off I reminisced of my takeoff from that same airport 45 years earlier, when I felt so relieved and thankful to have completed my missions in the CBI Theater and that I was heading home at last.

Driving along the road from the airport
to Kunming in 1989

Dave Hayward stands at the zero marker of the Burma Road in Kunming.

CHAPTER 35
A Veterans' Tour to China

IN THE FOLLOWING YEARS I made five more trips to China, all at the invitation and planning of the Chinese. The first such tour was in 2000, the next in 2004, two more in 2005, and another one in 2012.

The Hayward family was expanding. Our eldest son Gary Hayward and his wife Bobbi had a daughter, Courtney, and a son, Scott. Our son Eric Hayward and his wife Debbie had two sons, Brian and Nick. Kirk Hayward stayed single but joined me along with Eric and his son Nick on this next adventure. My wife Jeanne and Eric's other son Brian had responsibilities at home.

Seven members of the 22nd Bomb Squadron and family members took part in this return to China:

Ski and Tilley Bashinski
David, Kirk, Eric, and Nick Hayward
Wilmer, Rupert, and Trevor McDowell
Dick Pandorf
Jack Schofield
Bob and Elizabeth Selmer
Allen and Mary Ziehler

The 341st Bomb group was further represented by Bert Schwartz and Bill Smith of the 11th Bomb Squadron and by Leonard Logar of 341st Bomb Group headquarters.

Over 300 veterans, family members, and friends attended the "Sino-American WWII Veterans Reunion 2000" in China, April

23-30, 2000. The reunion was organized by Prof. Renjie Hua, President of the Beijing Aviators Association in conjunction with the Hump Pilots Association. We were taken care of royally by the Chinese government and military authorities at each of the well-planned tours and events. And we couldn't beat the price— $1,200 per person—plus for optional extensions—including all transportation, 4-star hotels, and all meals and scheduled tours.

On the afternoon of our arrival in Kunming, we joined in a group of 20 to see what was left of the old air base at Yangkai, getting a reminder of the countryside along the 2-hour route. The road was paved for most of the way. Families were seen swinging hoes to prepare rice paddies for the coming rains. Much of the land was planted in grain, the resulting straw used for making red bricks. I saw a few water buffalo lazily walking along the road.

Our van delivered us to the old airstrip at Yangkai. It was still intact, the site too well compacted for the planting of grain. Chinese security forces manned tents in one of the three remaining revetments (three-sided, square, dirt walls for protecting our airplanes from air attack). The airstrip seemed to be used now only as a roadway for farm equipment and animal transport.

The vans took us part way up the road to Red Dust Hill, the barracks area. I looked to the left to get another look at the airfield. To our right, amid trees, was where the base buildings had been, most of them having been removed and many of the trees cut down to provide more space for agriculture. Near where we stood was an abandoned building, a former social hall, according to our guide. Behind the building was a basketball court.

Returning to Kunming, we drove through Yangkai village, viewing once more the red-tile-roofed, red-mud-brick structures of the little town.

Back in Kunming we experienced one of those great Chinese dinners: a round table with a lazy-Susan in the center and with course after course of great food brought in generous quantities.

Little was the same in Kunming. Most of the old city had been demolished and new, high-rise hotels, apartments, and office buildings took their place along widened streets. The old Golden Horse Gate in Kunming was gone, a victim of street widening.

Some of Kunming seemed unchanged. The East and West Pagodas, dating from the Tang Dynasty, still rose majestically. Green Lake was now surrounded by a beautiful park. Nearby, the historic Yuantong Buddhist Temple from the Yuan Dynasty survived the Cultural Revolution.

Kirk, Eric, Nick and David Hayward at a golf course near the rest camp, in 2000

*Dick Pandorf and David Hayward inspected
the old airfield at Yangkai.*

Ruins of a social hall used by the airmen

Chapter 36
Return in 2004 and 2005

ANOTHER OPPORTUNITY TO VISIT China came up in 2004. Jeanne and I were invited to go there July 23rd to August 2nd. The invitation came from Jeff Greene and the Sino-American Aviation Heritage Foundation. Its purpose was to participate in the International Symposium on Sino-American Friendship in the Second World War. The symposium was composed of ten members. Three were from the American Volunteer Group (AVG), a B-25 pilot (myself), a P-51 pilot, a P-40 pilot, an Air Transport Command pilot, a China National Aviation Corporation pilot, and a Combat Cargo Command pilot. The entire trip was paid for by the Office of Information, Yunnan Province, China.

Our Chinese hosts were representatives of government, schools, universities, writers, television, and newspapers. The symposium was held at the Kai Wah Plaza International Hotel in Kunming, a 5-star hotel. Each member was asked to speak on the role he played with his type of airplane in China, his experiences in assisting the Chinese, and one or two exciting missions he flew. In addition, each member was asked to submit to interviews for the press and local TV stations, for the record.

I was picking up the pattern of what the Chinese really wanted to hear from returning veterans: How did we help the Chinese people during the war? That was something I could do, tell them of the contributions the B-25 squadrons made to the cause of China in World War II.

239

The Chinese treated us ten members like heroes who had rescued their country from the hands of the Japanese. This was unlike our experience in China in 1989 when, during our visit to Kweilin (now Guilin), where the B-25s of the 11th Bomb Squadron were stationed, our guide said to us, "There were never any Americans stationed here." At that time China still associated us with former leader Chiang Kai Shek. But now China recognized the help we rendered to their people in a time of need, and our hosts yearned to develop our friendship.

After the symposium concluded, our group of ten pilots plus wives and family were taken to points of interest in Kunming. The first was a photographic exhibit called "Yunnan in the Eyes of the Hump Flight Veterans." Again, photographers and interviewers were present to catch our reactions and comments as we viewed the pictures. Our second stop was the Hump Flight Memorial School. I reminded our hosts that the 22nd Bomb Squadron made a donation to this school in 1999 and I pointed out our squadron name engraved on a marble plaque in front of the school.

Some of us wanted to see Green Lake Park again, and the Buddhist Temple nearby. On Jinbi Lu Road we discovered the Hump Bar and saw many photos of World War II adorning its walls. Its owner was most interested in talking to us about old times, so I gave her a copy of our squadron book "WWII DIARY."

In 2005, I had two more chances to return to China; Jeff Greene arranged them again. The first was to Hong Kong and the second to Kunming and Zhijiang, to celebrate the 60th anniversary of the end of the war between China and Japan.

On August 14th I was in Hong Kong, China, after a comfortable flight in business class. Two other veterans were present, Mel McMullen of the 308th Bomb Group (B-24 heavy bombers) and Jimmie Adams, formerly a general and commanding officer of the 23rd Fighter Group. All expenses were paid by China.

We had two responsibilities. On August 16th we veterans were on stage for their 60th year celebration, while dignitaries made speeches and photographers snapped photos. On the 17th we were on stage again, this time before a group of university students, photographers, and dignitaries. We three told stories of helping the Chinese drive the invaders out of their country, followed by questions asked by the university students.

In addition to these events we were interviewed and photographed by the press. Jeff Greene put together a book of stories and photographs he compiled from previous interviews with returning veterans and the three of us autographed the book.

For relaxation, our hosts took us to Victoria Peak, Stanley Market, the Big Buddha on Landau Island, and the Jumbo Floating Restaurant.

After ten days at home, I was off to China again. My wife Jeanne joined us that time. Our group was comprised of 43 China veterans of World War II along with 47 family members. Representing the 22nd Bomb Squadron were Jack Schofield, Dick Pandorf, and me. Two of the Doolittle Raiders joined us: Dick Cole (Doolittle's copilot) and Tom Griffen (navigator). Dick Rossi, one of the original Flying Tigers, was with us also.

This trip, to celebrate the 60th anniversary of peace between China and Japan, took us to five cities in China. Zhijiang is the site of the Japanese laying down their arms in 1945 and coming to peace terms with China. You won't believe the welcome we had at the Zhijiang airport. Farmers came in from the countryside and lined the airport, just to see the arrival of the Flying Tigers. Hundreds of school children, dressed in their colorful uniforms, lined our path as we exited the airplane. They beat on drums, played on bugles and shouted, "Flying Tiger, Flying Tiger." When we left Zhijiang, the children were there again at 6:00 in the morning, hugging us, with tears in their eyes. It was truly an emotional experience. The three of us from the 22nd Bomb Squadron donated to the Flying Tigers Memorial at Zhijiang a copy of our squadron history book "Eagles, Bulldogs & Tigers," and we autographed the book for them.

At Nanjing we visited the Anti-Japanese Aviation Martyrs Monument. We observed the names of 22nd Bomb Squadron airmen who were killed in action, inscribed on the wall. Wilmer McDowell of our squadron had provided those names. I easily found Thomas J. Smith, Jr. and others from our squadron as well. The veterans placed flowers at the wall in memory of fallen comrades.

Arrival at Kunming welled up memories. We boarded cruise boats at Dianchi, the large lake just south of Kunming, and were taken to the site where salvage operations were under way to raise a P-40 that had crashed into the lake during World War II. We threw flowers into the lake at that site in memory of our departed friends.

At a banquet hosted by the Kunming municipal government, the veterans were each made honorary citizens, which entitled us to own property in Kunming if we choose to do so. We visited Yunnan University and fielded questions asked by the students. How bright and genuinely interested these students were about the history of the Flying Tigers, the Hump airlift, and the assistance our country gave to help the Chinese drive out the foreign invaders. On behalf of the 22nd Bomb Squadron, I gave the university copies of "The Bombing Bulldogs," "WWII DIARY," the videotape "Eagles, Bulldogs & Tigers in Action," and our embroidered squadron patches.

Top government men and women welcomed us in Beijing. We heard speeches from President and General Secretary Hu

Jintao and from Premier Wen Jiabao and dined at a table near the top ten leaders of China. It was an exhausting 17 days. As we lifted our tired bodies off the airplane in Los Angeles, we felt we had the experience of a lifetime.

In Hong Kong, David Hayward explained photos in the book prepared by Jeff Greene.

School children came out to welcome us at Zhijiang.

Jeanne found some friends at Zhijiang.

Dave Hayward explains the purpose of the stone roller—
to build airfields.

CHAPTER 37
My Sixth Return

MY SIXTH RETURN TRIP to China occurred in September 2012. We were a group of 27, including four veterans of the China-Burma-India Theater and 23 family members, or others having a special interest in coming on the tour.

Veteran Gary Tate worked with the railroad system that brought supplies from the ports of India to Assam Province, the jumping off spot for aerial supplies over the Hump to China. Another veteran, "Tex" Rankin, was a Hump pilot who flew 189 supply missions to China. Al Chinn rode one of the first truck convoys over the Ledo-Burma road to China and later manned a machine gun at the Kunming airport. I explained my role as pilot of a B-25 Mitchell bomber of the 22nd Bomb Squadron. We made up the foursome of veterans on this tour.

Our group met in Beijing on September 21, 2012, and the next day flew to Kunming. Our guide, Jeff Greene, was there to meet us, along with Mei Ying Deng to interpret. They had been our guides on previous tours to China. Jeff's knowledge of World War II history and Mei Ying's contact with Chinese people served us well.

Jeff explained to us the old airport at Kunming, which we knew so well, was abandoned and the new airport where we landed, about 30 miles east of Kunming, was just a few months old and truly a place of pride and beauty with most modern airport facilities.

We stayed at the luxurious Telecom International Hotel and visited the new China Telecom Museum. Indeed, CC-TV interviewers followed us everywhere we went. That night we "heroes" were welcomed at a banquet attended by local Chinese dignitaries and Telecom officials. The banquet was in celebration of the 70th Anniversary of the Hump Flights. Each veteran had a turn speaking to the group expressing gratitude for the hospitality they extended and our hopes for continued friendship with the Chinese people.

On Sunday morning we drove through the scenic hills north of Kunming to the Hump Flight Monument. As I climbed up the many stone steps to the monument location, I thought how much I appreciated the sturdy hand rails that were installed since my earlier visit. At the top, each veteran made a short speech of gratitude and recognition, while TV cameras recorded.

An hour later we stood on the old runway of now-abandoned Kunming Airport. I pointed out to the TV cameraman the grassy areas alongside the concrete runway where pilots were instructed to crash-land their planes if they were so badly shot up they would block the runway.

From there, we drove back to the new airport and departed westerly for Mangshi and then by bus to Ruili, along the Burma Road, an area occupied by the Japanese in World War II. The veterans told stories on the bus rides. I proudly told how the 22nd Bomb Squadron, in 1944, gave direct support to Chinese troops who fought to drive the Japanese invaders out of China's soil during the historic Salween River Campaign in that very area.

The next morning, Jeff Greene took us to the old American Volunteer Group (AVG Flying Tiger) airstrip at Loi Wing. P-40 shark-nosed fighter planes of the AVG were assembled and based there during the very early days of the war. Later, Loi Wing was captured by the Japanese and held until the Salween Campaign drove them out. Jeff told us that, beside him, we were the first Americans to set foot on the old airstrip since before the Japanese occupation.

From there we drove to the Wanting Bridge, where the Burma Road crosses from China into Burma. Burmese guards were there to prevent us from setting foot on Burma soil. TV cameramen came with us again to film and interview our people.

At dinner that night I sat next to the Mayor of Ruili, who spoke no English, but we had a nice visit by way of an interpreter. Jeff Greene advised us that in his several trips to this area he found no one who had any knowledge of the Salween campaign. People have moved on and town names have changed.

At Zhijiang, school children in their colorful uniforms met us, but not in the numbers we experienced previously. We were whisked to the Memorial Hall of Flying Tigers, featuring a wall of marble showing names of U.S. airmen killed in action in China, like the wall in Nanjing. I quickly found the name of Thomas J. "TJ" Smith of our squadron and explained to the group TJ's final mission. In the museum I saw on display a copy of the 22nd Bomb Squadron's history book "Eagles, Bulldogs & Tigers," which I had donated to the museum in 2005.

Continuing on our tour, we stopped at Nanjing. Our bus took us to Dr. Sun Yat Sen's Mausoleum and the Monument to the Air Martyrs in the war against Japan where 4,000 names of aviators are carved on tablets. I told our group that Wilmer McDowell of the 22nd Bomb Squadron was instrumental in providing the names of our squadron members who made the sacrifice.

A few days later, we thanked our hosts and departed for the U.S. It had been another memorable experience.

The veterans were hosted by Beijing Aviators Association. David Hayward is on the left.

The four veterans dedicated a wreath at the Hump Flight Monument.

*David Hayward stands at the Wanting Bridge, where the old
Burma Road crosses from China to Burma.*

*Grandson Brian Hayward was interviewed by
Chinese television.*

CHAPTER 38
What Happened to Them?

Loyal G. "LG" Brown lives with his wife Ruth in Midland, Michigan. Following his retirement from Dow Chemical Company, he devoted much of his time to local theater. At the Rapid City, South Dakota, reunion, LG and I flew that first mission of mine all over again. (See Chapter 1). LG was an early arrival at Chakulia, in a team who flew Lockheed Hudson bombers from the States for delivery to the Chinese. They were the first group of flyers to land at Ascension Island and  could not have made the crossing without that important refueling station.

John W. Boyd returned home to Mayfield, Kentucky, after release from the Japanese prison of war camp in Rangoon, Burma. He entered the real estate business, married, raised two daughters, was elected to the City Council of his town, and became Mayor. He organized the first reunion  of the 22nd Bomb Squadron and became known as the "father" of the 22nd Bomb Squadron Association. John remained active in the Association until he passed away in 2007.

General Claire L. Chennault organized the American Volunteer Group (AVG), bringing the first P-40 fighter planes and personnel to China before the U.S. entered World War II. After our entry, he became commanding officer of the Chinese American Task Force (CATF) and its  successor, the 14th Air Force, and achieved a remarkably successful record. He had an unfortunate falling out with General Stilwell and, late in the war, was relieved of his duties in China. Chennault retired in 1951 as a lieutenant general and died in 1958, with a most distinguished record.

Wayne M. Craven used his GI Bill of Rights benefits at the University of California, Berkeley, and then went on to medical school. After a successful 30-year medical practice, he retired in Bodega Bay, California, where he played golf and flew his own Bellanca airplane. He and his wife Lorraine produced five offspring. Wayne died  suddenly in 2004. Lorraine lives in Santa Rosa, California. Wayne and I went through flight training together and often flew together at Chakulia. Jeanne and I enjoyed visits to his lovely home at Bodega Bay as we remained the best of friends over the years.

James J. Hamer transferred to another unit and lost his life when a B-24 heavy bomber he was flying lost power on takeoff. He was my closest friend during flight training and at Chakulia. Jim's remains were cremated and in 1949 returned to the U.S. for burial at Forest Lawn Cemetery in Glendale, California. When I returned to the States, I called upon his family and expressed my sympathy.

Wendell H. Hanson was another good friend through training and overseas assignment, as well as after the war. His career was in the real estate business in Sioux Falls, South Dakota. He also served as a state senator in South Dakota. Wendell has been most supportive of the 22nd Bomb Squadron Association. He and his wife Helen

produced three sons and two daughters, of whom they are rightfully proud. Wendell and Helen live in Brandon, a suburb of Sioux Falls.

Thomas D. "Tom" Harmon flew into a thunderstorm while piloting a B-25 across the jungle of South America. He bailed out of the plane and, four days later, stumbled into civilization in Dutch Guiana. The rest of the crew did not get out. Determined to fly solo next time, he joined a P-38 squadron in China, but suffered another stroke of fate, shot down by a Japanese fighter plane in a dog fight over Japanese-occupied China. Badly burned, he bailed out. Friendly Chinese helped him return. Tom kept his parachute for his wife's wedding dress. He married Hollywood actress Elyse Knox. They had a son, Mark Harmon, who became quarterback for the UCLA Bruins and, later, a Hollywood actor. Tom was a sports announcer. At half time during a football game between Caltech and Pepperdine I went to the broadcast booth and said "Hello," not having seen him since we graduated from Williams Field, Arizona. Tom died of a heart attack in 1990.

David K. Hayward and his wife Jeanne live in Huntington Beach, California. Both are retired, Dave as a petroleum engineer and Jeanne as a school teacher. They have three sons, Gary, Eric, and Kirk and four grandchildren, Courtney, Scott, Brian, and Nickolas. Dave devotes much of his time to the business of the 22nd  Bomb Squadron and Jeanne to volunteer work at their church.

Stewart L. "Stew" Hayward, my brother, married Alice Storey. Their daughter Sandra was born in 1945 and a son Charles in 1948. Subsequently he had two more daughters, Nancy and Susan. Stew joined the U.S. Navy, assigned to the destroyer USS Putnam where he saw action at Leyte, Okinawa and Iwo Jima in the Western Pacific. After the war, he had a successful career as partner in a small  advertising firm. In 1963 he married Jo Ann Erikson and they moved to Newport Beach, California, where he served as commodore of the Shark Island Yacht Club. He retired from the Naval Reserve as a lieutenant commander. After a long illness, Stew passed away in 1996.

Melvin E. Heflinger was a boyhood friend who continued his flying as a captain with United Airlines. After mandatory retirement at age 60, he searched for one of the vintage Harlow PJC-2 airplanes, which were made by the aviation department at Pasadena Junior College when he attended. Mel found one in San Diego, restored it, and flew it. One day he landed in Huntington Beach and I went for a ride in it. Quite a thrill! Mel lived with his wife in Redondo Beach, California. He died in 2008.

John A. Johns was an in-house staff artist at the Pittsburgh Press, beginning in 1952. He drew caricatures and spot drawings, even created full color cover images, usually a current TV star, for magazines. In 1970 he left for a 30 year career as art instructor at the Art Institute of Pittsburgh, becoming its President for a decade. John contributed volumes of art work to 22nd Bomb Squadron Association publications. He passed away in 2005. This is one of my favorite drawings by John: "You are the wind beneath my wings."

General George C. Marshall became Secretary of State and, later, Secretary of Defense. He tried to broker a coalition government between the Chinese Nationalists and Communists, but the Chinese would not buy it. The general outlined a plan, known as the Marshall Plan, to restore Europe economically, and for that he received the Nobel Peace Prize. General Marshall passed away in 1959.

Wilmer E. "Wil" McDowell retired from the Air Force as a lieutenant colonel. He worked diligently with John Boyd to establish the 22nd Bomb Squadron Association and its reunions that followed, serving as the association's first president. Wilmer died in 2001 at age 83, but not before returning to China with our tour group  in 2000. His daughter Lucy and son Rupert have been most helpful in carrying on the tradition of the squadron, with Lucy working on membership and Rupert on reunions.

Charles Wesley "Wes" Parlee, my best friend during boyhood, used his GI Bill benefit to attend Art Center College of Design in Pasadena, California, leading to a career in commercial art with the County of Los Angeles. While employed there, Wes met Verna who would become his wife  and, together, they raised a nice family. They spent much of their time at their chalet at Big Bear Lake, where Jeanne and I often visited. Wes set up a studio in the upper floor of the chalet, with its ideal skylight, and continued with his paintings. It was a sad day for me when I attended his funeral in 2004.

Jack L. Schofield, a pilot with the 22nd Bomb Squadron, joined the veterans returning to China in 2000 and 2005. His career was in teaching and politics, having served Nevada as both a state assemblyman and state senator. At present he is a member of the Board of Regents of the  University of Nevada. Jack and his wife of many years, Alene, produced a large, devoted family in the Mormon tradition. His devotion to teaching in the field of mathematics and science led to the City of Las Vegas naming a middle school after him. Jack achieved his first degree from University of Utah, where in September 2013, he was honored with a College of Science Distinguished Alumni Award. He earned his Doctorate in Education degree from the University of Nevada at age 72. Jack and his wife live in Las Vegas.

Bradley C. Stewart, another boyhood friend, moved to the San Francisco Bay area after World War II and from there I lost all contact with him. Efforts to restore contact were not successful.

General Patrick W. Timberlake, with whom I flew many times at Bolling Field, was in charge of the 9th Bomber Command in North Africa prior to his move to Washington. In North Africa he flew the B-25 and wanted to be the pilot on most of our trips together. After World War II he was assigned to Okinawa and finally was in command of Allied Air Forces in Southern Europe, based in Naples. He retired as a lieutenant general in 1957 and died in San Antonio, Texas, in 1983 at age 81.

CHAPTER 39
Closing Comments

AT MY AGE OF 91 all my boyhood friends are gone and only one close friend from China-Burma-India remains—Wendell Hanson—my "twin," in his words. The Good Lord has been kind to me and my family.

Memories of the CBI are kept alive through my work as secretary-treasurer of the 22nd Bomb Squadron Association. Our squadron newsletters and the web site are important vehicles in that respect. I am still in contact with 54 veterans of the 22nd Squadron, of which there were 1,132 recorded members during three years of World War II. Our newsletters go out to those veterans and their remaining families and other people at interest—170 total. Recently I received this email:

My father, Ralph Fiske, was a member of the 22nd during WWII. He passed away several years ago, but I found your web page, and living near Savannah now, I was interested in the reunion and ordering some pins for my children, sisters, and nephews and nieces. Any information would be appreciated and I thank you for all your service to our country. Gail Fiske Bethea.

Gail's email brought back flashes of memory: "Bucky" Fiske living in our basha, his captaincy, appointment to provost marshal to earn his extra pay, the stolen safe and his effort to find the thieves, that mission when a weatherman aboard wanted to go "just a little bit further" to study the weather, not enough fuel to make it back to base, and bailing out of the plane. At Santa Monica I learned Bucky and his crew returned safely to Yangkai. I responded to Gail:

> Thank you for your email and finding our website. I knew your father well. We called him "Bucky." He lived in our basha in India and I was concerned when he and his crew had to bail out in Indochina. I kept in contact with his bombardier, Jim Sullivan, for many  years. We have a few lapel pins left. Come to our reunion and you can see them.

Gail wrote back:

> So great to hear from you and find out that you knew my father, "Bucky" to his friends and family. It brought tears to my eyes. He was a wonderful husband and father and adored by his three daughters. He was in touch with Sully (Jim Sullivan) through the years. I look forward to meeting you in Savannah. It will be an honor to speak with you. Thank you again.

Acknowledgments

I wish to express my gratitude to all those who influenced me in putting this book together:

My father Sumner M. Hayward and brother Stewart L. Hayward who stood by me and my plans to serve my country in the way I did.

Mr. Grinstead, my Economics teacher at Pasadena Junior College, who gave me further encouragement.

My boyhood friends, Wesley Parlee and Bradley Stewart. We three developed the common interest and determination to enter the aviation cadet program for pilot training in the Army Air Corps.

My flight instructors: Mr. D. L. Chapman and Lieutenants Dorris, Grumman, and Kempster.

Close friends I made in the service: Jim Hamer, Wendell Hanson, Wayne Craven, and others.

My basha-mates at Chakulia: Jim Hamer, Bill Dempsey, Jim Sullivan, Wayne Craven, Bucky Fiske, Art Lynch, and Tom Dunham.

Seasoned pilots who guided me through my indoctrination to combat operations: Loyal G. "LG" Brown and Patrick L. Ham.

Storyteller Steve Stankiewicz and caricaturist John A. Johns.

263

John M. Boyd and Wilmer E. McDowell, who established the 22nd Bomb Squadron Association and the plan for reunions to follow.

As my family developed, much gratitude goes to my wife Jeanne, who tolerated my arising at 5:00 am to write down a new thought or revision in preparing this book. Jeanne organized our trip to China in the year 1989 and also joined me on veterans' trips to China in 2004 and 2005.

Our three fine sons, Gary, Eric, and Kirk, who have been an encouragement as well. Eric, Kirk, and Eric's sons, Brian and Nicholas, accompanied me on return trips to China. Kirk has been a great help in organizing and editing this book. My sister-in-law, Jo Ann Hayward, and Jeanne's cousin, Laurie Jones, have contributed to many of our reunions.

Jeff Greene, a most helpful organizer of my return trips to China in 2004, 2005, and 2012.

Rupert "Rupe" McDowell, our reunion chairman, with whom I worked to plan and carry out annual reunions of the 22nd Bomb Squadron Association. At those reunions, I developed new friends from the 22nd Bomb Squadron, including Dick Pandorf, Jack Schofield, and others.

Captain Daniel Jackson, an Air Force Academy graduate, who wrote: "I'm glad you are writing about your experiences. I think it's important both for the world and for your family."

Sources

The author's personal records:
  My 1942 diary
  Individual Flight Record
  Photograph collection
  Previously written articles
  Military orders and letters
Governmental records:
  Official records of the 22nd Bomb Squadron at
      Maxwell Air Force Base, Alabama
  National Archives and Records Administration,
      College Park, Maryland
Publications of the 22nd Bomb Squadron Association:
  Book: "Eagles, Bulldogs & Tigers"
  Book: "WWII DIARY"
  Quarterly newsletters
  DVD: "The History of Reunions, 22nd Bomb
      Squadron Association"

CPSIA information can be obtained at www.ICGtesting.com
Printed in the USA
BVOW04s1659030214

343651BV00002B/49/P